Celebrating Wiccan Spirituality

Spells, Sacred Rites, and Folklore for Each Day of the Year

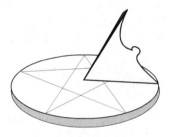

By

Lady Sabrina

NEW PAGE BOOKS
A division of The Career Press, Inc.
Franklin Lakes, NJ

CELEBRATING WICCAN SPIRITUALITY
EDITED BY NICOLE DEFELICE
TYPESET BY EILEEN DOW MUNSON
Cover design by Diane Y. Chin
Printed in the U.S.A. by Book-mart Press

To order this title, please call toll-free 1-800-CAREER-1 (NJ and Canada: 201-848-0310) to order using VISA or MasterCard, or for further information on books from Career Press.

The Career Press, Inc., 3 Tice Road, PO Box 687,
Franklin Lakes, NJ 07417
www.careerpress.com
www.newpagebooks.com

Library of Congress Cataloging-in-Publication Data

Sabrina, Lady.
    Celebrating Wiccan spirituality : spells, sacred rites, and folklore for each day of the year / by Lady Sabrina.
        p. cm.
    Includes bibliographical references and index.
    ISBN 1-56414-593-X (pbk.)
        1. Witchcraft—Calendars. I. Title

    BF1572.F37 S23 2002
    299—dc21

                                                                                2002071910

To my sister Sharon and my Dad. And to Aristaeus, Autumn, Damaclease, and Balaam.

I would like to thank Mike Lewis, Nicole DeFelice, Stacey Farkas, and the New Page staff, who always do such a great job.

Contents

Introduction

Celebrating Wiccan Spirituality is a magickal journey through the ritual of the year. It introduces the folklore associated with calendar customs and festivals, some of which are integral to the Wiccan religion, and others to our secular lifestyles. Although most of the traditional holidays that Wiccans celebrate originated from ancient religious practices, some are fresh attempts to recreate a sense of community and reconnect with Nature.

Not all of the holidays within these pages are profoundly spiritual. In fact, many are just simple reminders of what it means to be human and face the day-to-day rigors of mundane life. This was something our ancestors learned when they gave up hunting and gathering and began to plant crops. Suddenly, hard work and the influence of the seasons took on a deeper and more significant meaning. Winter, Spring, Summer, and Fall brought forth want, promise, fulfillment, and hopefully harvest. It was no wonder that our ancestors viewed the waning of the sun with considerable foreboding, because the barren landscape seemed to last forever.

For those who lived off the land, life was an endless struggle of long hours of backbreaking work with very little, if any, time for recreation. When they did manage to squeeze out a few moments of leisure, it was usually for religious or family outings. In our modern society, filled with every time-saving device imaginable, it is hard to imagine how these early pioneers managed—let alone survived. But survive they did, leaving us with a rich and abundant tapestry of unique folklore, festivals, and celebrations that pays homage to humanity's creativity and ability to make the most of every situation.

Today, we still celebrate the seasonal changes, as well as other festivals that allow us to take advantage of the potential emanating from the earth. The planet's rotation, gravitational pull, and astrological configurations change with each season, producing different levels of energy that can be harnessed and channeled to magickally manifest a personal goal.

Besides being a good time to project for personal gain, seasonal celebrations provide us with the opportunity to make new friends and create lasting traditions. Whether they are secular or religious, holidays bring people together. They provide us with a time to meet in celebration, as well as in prayer, and help us gain a deeper understanding of ourselves and those who travel life's path with us.

Suggestions for Using This Book

Take a few moments to scan through the book and familiarize yourself with its format. If you have any special days of your own coming up, you might want to check those dates first. If there is anything special you need to acquire, you will have time to get it. For example: Your daughter's birthday falls on February 5 and you see that the magickal activity for that day is crystal gazing. This is the kind of activity that could be used to enhance her party, making it that much more special.

January

January derives its name from the ancient Roman god Janus—the two-faced divinity of beginnings and endings. He was the gatekeeper of heaven, and the guardian of the gateways, who looked simultaneously forward and backward. Janus was held in high regard and considered the source of all things. The ups and downs of fortunes, the civilization of the human race, and the changing of the seasons were all under his dominion. Just like its namesake, January looks forward to the new year as it reflects back on the old—the concept of new possibilities arising from past conditions.

Mentally, January is the month of regeneration and recreation when time is abolished and starts again. It is that month when we all make resolutions to change—to leave the past behind and start anew.

In medieval England and parts of Scotland, preparations for the new year included house cleaning and fumigation. Everything was swept, scrubbed, raked, and changed. Entryways were freshly painted, new window coverings were hung, and old furnishing were recovered or replaced. This massive cleaning was done to get rid of any lingering malevolent spirits, and hopefully prevent their return.

Magickal Themes for January:

New beginnings, resolutions, planning

Magickal Correspondences:

Colors: White, silver, blue

Foods: Marzipan, fish, cheese, red wine, sweet cakes

Plants: Sage, thyme, verbena, juniper, bay

Stones: Aquamarine, blue lace agate, pearl, jet

Symbols: Janus, silver coins, hour glass

Full Moon: Wolf Moon

1 January
New Year's Day

Pray don't 'ee wash on New Year's day,
or you'll wash one of the family away.
Cast holy water all about,
And have a care no fire goes out.
—Robert Herrick (1591–1674)
The New Year's Gift

The first day of the New Year was sacred to *Jupiter* and *Juno,* the Roman equivalent of the Greek Zeus and Hera. This day also celebrated the power of *Gamelia,* the fortuitous side, or aspect, of Hera. All things that concern luck and love were overseen by Gamelia, especially marriages.

New Year's Day has always been considered a time of omens and portents. It was (and still is) believed that everything you do on this day will influence your luck for the coming year. Nothing should be taken from the house this day—not even rubbish. If it is absolutely necessary to put anything out, be sure to bring something back in first, preferably a coin concealed outside the night before.

Magickal Activity
A New Year Prosperity Amulet

Items needed: One new silver coin; a small blue bag; one whole fresh or dried sage leaf; one 6-inch length of silver ribbon.

Place the coin and sage leaf in the blue bag. Tie the bag shut with the silver ribbon. Use the following chant to activate the amulet:

> *Silver and Sage, on this first day of the year,*
> *Favor me always with wealth and good cheer.*

Hang the charged amulet from the mirror in your car, or carry it to attract prosperity and happiness.

2 January
Advent of Isis

In ancient Egypt this day was set aside to honor the Goddess Isis, the *Queen of Sorcery, Mother of the Moon*, and *Life of the Nile*. At this time a ceremony known as the *Advent of Isis* was performed to honor the Goddess who brought civilization, peace, and prosperity to all of Egypt.

To the Egyptians Isis was the female principle of Nature—the Goddess of 1,000 names. She was revered as *"the great magician"* who protected her son Horus from predators and other dangers. Because she protected her son, many believed she would protect mortal children from the perils of daily life as well.

Magickal Activity
Isis Protection Spell

Items needed: A picture or representation of the Goddess Isis; and one white candle.

Set the picture of Isis on a small table, and place the candle in front of it. Light the candle and focus your attention on the picture as you recite this simple prayer:

> *Great Goddess Isis*
> *I beseech Thee alone.*
> *To bless and protect,*
> *My family and home.*

Leave the candle to burn for one hour. This spell may be repeated any time you feel the need for protection.

3 January
St. Genevieve, the Deer Dance, and Weather Forecasting

In the *East Anglian* tradition this day was dedicated to St. Genevieve, patroness of the city of Paris. At seven years of age

Genevieve was singled out of a crowd by St. Germain of Auxerre, who foretold of her future sanctity. The life of St. Genevieve was one of great austerity, constant prayer, and works of charity.

January 3 is still the day that Native American tribes of the Pueblo perform their annual fertility ceremony, known as the *Deer Dance*. This centuries-old ceremony includes a ritual dance performed by a Shaman, wearing a deer headdress, who invokes the Goddess known as the Deer Mother. When properly summoned, the Deer Mother grants the tribe prosperity for the coming year.

In Elizabethan England, the third day of January was set aside to observe the weather. It was believed that if the weather was mild at this time, it would be paid for later. This rhyme, from *The Perpetual Almanack of Folklore* by Charles Kightly, is an example of this observance:

> *A kindly good Janiveer,*
> > *Freezeth the pot by the fire.*
> *If in January, the sun much appear,*
> > *March and April pay full dear.*

❋

4 January
Sacrifice to the 7 Stars

The ancient Greeks set this day aside to honor Callisto, the moon Goddess who was loved by Zeus. Callisto bore Zeus a son, *Arcas*, and was then changed into a bear either by Zeus, wishing to hide her, or by Hera herself. As a bear she was shot by Artemis in the forest, who then placed her among the stars as the *She Bear* connected with the Ursa Major constellation.

In Greek Callisto was also called Helice, which means both "that which turns" and "Willow branch"—a reminder that the willow was the sacred tree favored by Helice and Callisto.

Magickal Activity
The Willow Wand

To make the wand: Cut a small branch from a Willow tree. Clean and sand the branch until it is smooth. Use silver paint to inscribe your name in a spiral pattern around the branch.

Use a smudge stick to consecrate your wand. Light the smudge, and pass the wand through its fragrant smoke. This will remove any negative thoughts or vibrations that might have been attached to the branch before you acquired it.

Once the branch has been cleansed you will need to bless it in Callisto's honor. Place the wand on your altar or on a small table. Hold both of your hands over the wand and speak the following prayer:

> *Goddess of the moon grant to me,*
> *The Willows power of flexibility.*
> *Through your love I shall be warmed,*
> *And from this moment be transformed.*

When you feel the need to be more flexible and accommodating, hold your wand and repeat the prayer.

5 January
Eve of the Feast of the Epiphany

This 11th day of Christmas is dedicated to the Italian fairy-Goddess *Befana*. Although they are rapidly disappearing, many of the customs associated with this day are still held, especially in rural-Italian farming areas. At sunset, an effigy of Befana is placed on a stack of brushwood, which is then burned. If the smoke blows to the east, it is believed that the year will be filled with prosperity and abundance.

Reminiscent of our Christmas Eve, Italian children put out stockings on this night in hopes that Befana will fill them with presents while the adults write their wishes on pieces of paper. The papers are then tossed in the hearth where they catch fire and float up the chimney, granting the petitioners wish.

Magickal Activity
Hearth Blessing

Items needed: A broom; one 3-foot length of natural cord; one white 3-wick candle.

Place the candle on a table near the hearth along with the broom and the piece of cord. The entire family should gather around the table. The head of the household will step forward, light each candle wick, and say:

> *I bring light to this home, I bring love to this home,*
> *I bring honor to this home.*

In turn, each member of the household will then tie a knot in the cord. The last person to tie a knot in the cord will then tie the cord around the handle of the broom. He or she will pass the broom to the mother of the household, who will symbolically sweep all of the negative energies away from the hearth while chanting:

> *All that is evil is now swept away,*
> *And nothing but good shall come this way.*

The broom should then be placed next to the hearth. The candle is left to burn for one hour and extinguished. Each evening, the head of the household will light the candle in Befana's honor to ensure peace and harmony within the home.

6 January
Twelfth Night, Epiphany of Kore, and Persephone

Traditionally, on this day the ancient Greeks would carry the statue of Kore around her temple seven times as they prayed for protection and good fortune. Following the temple activities a nocturnal rite was held in honor of Kore (daughter of Zeus and Demeter, whose name means "maiden"), an aspect of Persephone before her marriage to Hades.

On this day in Old Europe the ashes from the Yule log were removed, and either stored for magickal purposes or scattered on the fields to insure fertility. Later on in the day the *Lord of Misrule,* known as the King of the Bean, was selected. Cakes were made, and a bean was baked into one. Whomever found the bean in his cake was then elected king for the day. The king, along with the Queen of the Pea (selected by finding the pea baked into another batch of cakes) ruled over the final Yuletide festivities.

Magickal Activity
King and Queen Buttermilk Clove Cake

3 cups flour

2 tsp. ground cloves

1 tsp. ground cinnamon

1 cup butter, softened

2 eggs

1½ cups buttermilk

1 dried pea

1½ tsp. baking soda

¼ tsp. ground allspice

½ tsp. ground nutmeg

1½ cups light brown sugar

1 egg yolk

1 dried bean

Sift the flour with the baking soda and spices. In a large bowl, beat butter, brown sugar, eggs, and egg yolk at high speed for about 5 minutes. At low speed, beat the flour mixture in fourths alternately with the buttermilk in thirds. Beat for 1 minute only. Pour the batter into two greased and floured 9" x 1" layer pans. Push the bean into one cake and the pea into the other. Bake at 350 degrees for 25 to 30 minutes. Cool 10 minutes in pans, then remove to serving plates.

To choose the king and queen, place the cake with the bean in it on a table for the gentlemen. The cake with the pea is left in the kitchen for the ladies. The men eat their cake first. When one has been acknowledged as the king, the women will then partake of their cake to determine who will be the queen.

7 January
Saint Distaff's Day

In southern England, Saint Distaff's Day was when work began again after the Christmas holiday. Saint Distaff's Day was not a saint's day at all, but rather a tongue-in-cheek commemoration of the day on which women returned to their distaffs of unspun wool.

8 January
Justitia's Day (Themis)

In classical Paganism, the spirit of Justice was feminine. It was believed that the quality of justice depended upon the *feminine principle of Nature,* which had a closer kinship with *natura justum* (that which is by Nature) than the masculine sex had.

It was Themis, the daughter of Uranus and Gaea and advisor to Zeus, who personified law and order. She protected the innocent, punished the guilty, and was considered the Goddess of law, peace, justice, and righteousness. Themis carried a set of scales and was present at all feasts, social gatherings, and oath-swearing ceremonies.

Magickal Activity
Prayer for Justice
Gracious Goddess, I beseech thy advocacy on my behalf. Give to those who judge the spirit of wisdom and understanding that they may discern the truth. Allow them to render justice moderated with compassion and mercy.

9 January
Festival of Jana and Janus

On this day the ancient Romans honored *Jana*, whose name means "luminous sky," and her husband *Janus*, the guardian of all passageways. At their festival, a ram was sacrificed to Janus for his continued protection, and Jana was invoked to shine her light on the new year. To the Romans, who believed that the spirit of Janus hovered over all doorways, gates, and passageways, this was a time of great consequence.

10 January
Plough Monday

In rural Europe the first Monday after the Twelfth Day of Christmas was Plough Monday and was considered to be the beginning of the agricultural year. Very little work was done on this day. Instead, a plough was decorated and dragged around the fields and through the streets of the village while its bearers begged for money. Anyone who refused to participate was in danger of having his or her garden ploughed up.

The money the participants collected was used to purchase a large candle. This was then placed on the altar in the village church. The candle would then be blessed by the presiding priest to ensure good weather for ploughing and an abundant harvest.

Magickal Activity
New Year Success Spell

Items needed: One yellow beeswax candle; green ribbon;
a small piece of parchment paper.

To begin, inscribe your name near the top of the candle, and then tie the green ribbon around its base. Write out your wish for the coming year on the piece of paper. Place the candle in a holder and set it on top of the paper. Light the candle and chant the following seven times:

> *Busy as can be,*
> > *Bright as a light.*
> *The success I see,*
> > *Is mine from this night.*

Allow the candle to burn for one hour and then extinguish. Repeat this spell for seven days, each day allowing the candle to burn for one hour. On the seventh day the candle is allowed to burn out. You will then want to fold the parchment paper into a small packet, secure with the green ribbon, and carry on your person.

11 January
Roman Festival of Carmentalia/
English Hogmanay

In ancient Rome the festival of *Carmentalia* was held to honor the nymphs of prophecy who were known as the *Camenae*. The principal nymph was Carmenta, the Goddess of prophecy who protected women in childbirth. Pregnant women would offer Carmenta rice and fresh vegetables in exchange for a safe delivery. Those women wishing to have children would ask Carmenta to bless wild berries that they would then eat to internalize fertility.

Magickal Activity
Ring on a String

If you, or someone you are close to, is pregnant this is an auspicious time to predict the sex of the child. Take a gold ring and suspend it from a chain or string and hold it over the mother's belly. Should the string move in a circular motion it signifies that the baby is a girl. If, on the other hand, it swings back and forth the baby will surely be a boy.

In old English folklore the 11th of January was Hogmanay, the day after Christmas, when Witches were supposed to become active again. The York Castle Trial Records of January 11, 1655, revealed the following charm to ward off bewitchment of cattle:

> *Put a pair of breeches upon the cow's head, and beat her out of the pasture with a good cudgel upon a Friday, and she will run to the Witch's door and strike threat with her horns.*
> —Reginald Scott,
> *The Discovery of Witchcraft*, 1584

12 January
Compitalia (Lares and Penates)

To the ancient Romans, the *Lares* and *Penates* were synonymous with ancestral ghosts or spirits. Every family had its own Lare that protected the home and several Penates who watched over the hearth and food pantry.

Typically, the Lare was a small bronze statuette of a youthful figure holding a dish and raising a drinking horn. It was housed in a small shrine or niche in the wall and was prayed to each morning and at mealtime. During special family events (births, birthdays, weddings, and deaths) the little figurine was crowned, decorated with flower garlands, and given offerings of incense, cakes, and wine.

The festival of *Compitalia* was held in honor of the Lares and marked the end of the agricultural year. Shrines erected at the crossroads *(compita)* where three or four farms intersected. A broken plowshare was hung up at the shrine, and an altar was set up for sacrifice. There would be a blessing rite that was followed by a period of feasting. It was Augustus who transformed the rural celebration of Compitalia into a state festival that was conducted by a state priest on behalf of all the people.

Magickal Activity
The Lare Shrine for Household Protection

Items needed: One small wall shelf; a figurine to represent the Lare; a small dish; one white votive candle in a glass holder; a sprig of Rue; a stick of sandalwood incense and ash catcher; a small bowl of salt; a glass of water.

Hang the shelf in the kitchen at eye level. Place the Lare, dish, candle, and sprig of Rue on the shelf.

On the first Saturday morning following the full moon of January, consecrate your shrine as follows:

Begin by placing three pinches of salt into the glass of water. Dip the sprig of Rue into the salt water and sprinkle the mixture over the shrine while you say:

> *May the power of salt and water combine,*
> *To bless and consecrate this sacred shrine.*

Light the candle, and the incense stick while you say:

> *I now beckon the spirits of the hearth and home,*
> *To make your presence to me now known.*
> *Bless and protect all that you can see,*
> *For this I shall reward you, so mote it be.*

The shrine has now been activated. Each morning offer the Lare a piece of your food. On decorate your shrine with seasonal flowers and foods. Light the candle and the incense, and thank the Lare for his protection.

13 and 14 January
Midvintersblot/Saint Hilary's Day

Midvintersblot or Midwinter's offering, often called Tiugunde Day in Old England, was sacred to *Tiu*, the ancient Teutonic chief God and ruler of the year. This festival falls 20 days after Yule and is when the runic half-month of Peorth commences.

This day was christianized as Saint Hilary's day (for Hilary of Poitiers), the patron of backward children, who was invoked against snake bites. This time is traditionally the coldest point of the year and marks the time when marriages were once again permitted after the Christmas season.

15 January

According to *The Perpetual Almanack of Folklore* by Charles Kightly, from the *Markham County Contentments* (1615), this day was reserved for taking care of one's hounds. It seems that when the hounds were done with the hunt, one was to immediately wash the animals' feet in hot butter and beer, beef broth, or a brew of mallows and nettles. Once properly cleansed, the hounds were to be allowed to rest before the fire for several hours. When the hounds were rested and refreshed, they would be rousted and turned out to find their own housing.

16 January
Concordia

To the ancient Romans, the Goddess Concordia was the personification of *concord* (an agreement between members of the state or between members of groups within a guild) and sometimes associated with the Greek Goddess Homonoia— the incarnation of harmony.

On this day, considered to be the center-post of the first month of the new year, Concordia was petitioned to help with the formation of favorable partnerships with business as well as with love and friendships.

Magickal Activity
Circle of Friendship Spell

Items needed: One pink candle for each person you wish to befriend; one gold candle to represent yourself; one sprig of rosemary; one sprig of lavender.

Begin by placing each pink candle, evenly spaced, in a circle. In the center of the circle lay the rosemary and lavender sprigs in a cross formation. Place the gold candle next to the center of the cross. Take a few moments to relax. Visualize yourself and your circle of friends having a wonderful time.

Light the gold candle first, and then in a clockwise direction light each of the pink candles. Chant the following once for each friendship candle:

> *As the stars above in darkness shine,*
> *With a light that fills the heavens divine.*
> *So bright with radiance our friendships glow,*
> *Outshining the sun and dimming all foes.*

Allow the candles to burn for one hour and then extinguish. Repeat the spell every evening until the candles have burned out. Save the rosemary and lavender. It can be used later for friendship amulets.

17 January
Wassailing

This was the proper time for Wassailing in the apple grow-ing regions of southern and western England. Large parties gathered in the orchards by night to sing to the trees, drink to their health, and pour cider over their roots. Pieces of toast were soaked in cider and then placed on the branches of the trees for the guardian birds. Near midnight horns were blown and guns fired, and everyone would give a great howl to frighten off any angry or evil spirits that might blight the crop.

Old apple tree, we wassail thee, and hoping thou wilt bear,
For the Lord doth know, where we shall be,
till apples come another year.
To bear well, to bloom well, so merry let us be,
Let every man take off his hat and
shout to the old apple tree.
Old apple tree, we wassail thee, and hoping thou wilt bear,
Hats full, cups full, three-bushel bags full,
And a little heap under the stairs.
        —Charles Kightly,
          Pererpetual Almanack of Folklore

18 January
Festival of Perth

In Australia this day was dedicated to the Aborigine Mother Goddess Nungeena. According to her legend, evil spirits destroyed the earth with insects. Nugeena then created the most beautiful birds of all: lyre birds. These magnificent creatures in turn made other birds, who assisted with the work of clearing away the insects and restoring the world to its original beauty.

Magickal Activity
Feather and Cord Healing Spell

Items needed: One 36-inch piece of white cord; seven feathers, one each of the following colors: red, orange, yellow, green, blue, indigo, and violet; a photograph of the person being healed.

Place the picture on a table or shelf so that it is at eye level. Concentrate on the picture and see in your mind's eye the person overcoming his or her illness. Begin by saying the following prayer:

> *Great Goddess Nungeena on this hour,*
> *Allow me to be your channel of power.*
> *Let your forces now work through me,*
> *For this I will so shall it be.*

Visualize the person you wish to heal. Begin by tying each feather, red, orange, yellow, green, blue, indigo, and violet (evenly spaced), into the cord as you chant:

> *By the knot of one, this spell has now begun.*
> *By the knot of two, I shall now heal you.*
> *By the knot of three, I give healing power to thee.*
> *By the knot of four, you are strengthened ever more.*
> *By the knot of five, you will now begin to thrive.*

By the knot of six, your illness I now fix.
With this knot of seven, your illness is gone,
*   you are now healthy, from this moment on.*

To complete the spell, wrap the cord and feathers around the person's picture and store in a safe place.

19 January
The Tarbh-Feis

The Tarbh-Feis, or Bull Prophecy, was performed by the ancient Druids to seek the help of the spirits. A bull was slaughtered, and its hide was removed. One of the Druids would then wrap himself in the bloody side of the hide and lay down upon a bed of rowan-wattle. During his sleep or trance, the visions or dreams he had were taken as prophecy. The knowledge he gained from the dream was used for the betterment of the king and community.

20 and 21 January
St. Agnes's Eve and St. Agnes's Day

St. Agnes was a Roman Catholic child martyr who was beheaded in the year 304 A.D. for refusing to marry. Her eve has traditionally been a time for lovers' divination—especially divination by fire. One very old custom tells: To be sure to dream of your future husband tonight, fast strictly and keep silent all day. On no account allow anyone—not even a child—to kiss you. At bedtime you must dress in your finest night-dress, then boil an egg. When the egg is hard, take out the yolk, fill the space with salt, and eat the egg, shell and all. Then walk backwards to bed while saying:

> *Fair St. Agnes, play thy part,*
> *And send to me my own sweetheart.*
> *Not in his best or worse array,*
> *But in the clothes he wears every day.*

You will then surely dream of your intended, but tell no one of your dream or the spell will be broken.

Magickal Activity
Visions of Love Spell

Items needed: One dram of pure rose oil; one bowl of water; one pink birthday candle.

Place the bowl of water on the night stand next to your bed. Sprinkle seven drops of the rose oil into the bowl. Turn all the lights off in the room. Light the pink candle. Hold the candle over the bowl so the wax will fall onto the water, and chant the following seven times:

> *Rose and water,*
> > *Flame and fire,*
> *Reveal this night,*
> > *The one I desire.*

As soon as the candle has burned out, close your eyes and go to sleep. When you awake in the morning, the name of the one you will marry will be spelled out in the wax drippings left in the bowl.

22 January
St. Vincent's Day/ Festival of Apollo

St. Vincent, deacon and first Spanish martyr, was widely venerated during the Middle Ages. This day has long served to watch the weather and the legs, which are ruled by Aquarius.

> *Remember on St. Vincent's day,*
> *If that the Sun his beams display.*
> *For 'tis a token, bright and clear,*
> *Of prosperous weather all the year.*

In ancient Greece this day was dedicated to Apollo, the Sun God of light, poetry, and oracles. It was believed that if one carried his emblem (pictured here) good luck, light, and truth would follow. Hesperides wrote "To Apollo: A Short Hymne" (1648) to honor Apollo on this day:

> *Thou mighty Lord, and master of the lyre,*
> *Unshorn Apollo, come, and re-inspire,*
> *My fingers so, the Lyrick-strings to move*
> *That I may play, and sing a Hymne of Love.*

23 January
Day of Hathor

On this date, the annual Egyptian festival of Hathor took place. Hathor (Greek for Athyr), meaning *the dwelling of Horus,* was the patroness of women, a mistress of merriment and sovereign of music and dance. Her temples were a home of intoxication and a place of enjoyment. In addition to being a Goddess of joy and love, Hathor watched over the dead. She bore the title of "Queen of the West," where she would wait in the foliage of the sycamore tree, at the edge of the desert, and welcome the dead with bread and water.

Magickal Activity
Love-Drawing Bath

Sprinkle ¼ cup fresh rose petals and ¼ cup fresh lavender buds into your bath water. While soaking in the herbal water chant the following:

> *Let true love now come to me,*
> *For this I will so mote it be.*

Stay in the tub for 15 minutes and meditate on the type of person you wish to attract.

24 January
St. Paul's Eve

It was at this time that St. Paul was converted from a Roman persecutor to a member of the Christian faith. Due to the profound atmospheric conditions at that time, St. Paul's Eve became a time of great importance, and a weather omen for the coming year:

> *If the day of St. Paul's proves clear,*
> *Then shall betide a happy year.*
> *If it chance to snow or rain,*
> *Then shall be dear all kinds of grain.*
> *But if high winds shall be aloft,*
> *Wars shall vex this realm full oft.*
> *And if thick mists make dark the sky,*
> *Both beasts and fowl this year shall die.*
> —Erra Pater, 1694

25 and 26 January
Old Disting/Burns Night

On the old runic calendars the 25th and 26th of January were for *Disting*—the feast of *Disir* the Norse guardian Goddess. Great festivals were held in her honor at the temple in Uppsala, Sweden.

In more recent times it has become Burns Night, celebrating the birthday (1759) of the 18th-century Scottish bard Robert Burns. Traditionally friends and family gather for an evening of poetry, music, and feasting on Haggis.

> *Fair fa' your honest sonsie face*
> *Great Chieftain o' the pudden race*
> *Abune them a' ye tak your place*
> *Painch, tripe, or thairm*

Wheel are ye worthy o' agrace
As lang's my airm
—Burns Address to Haggis

27 January
Day of Ishtar

In ancient Babylon, Ishtar was acknowledged as the "Light of the World" and the Goddess of the morning and evening. Her symbols were an eight-pointed star and crescent moon. She was divine personification of the planet Venus and the dispenser of the *Never-Failing Waters of Life.* Fertility and all aspects of creation were her epiphany.

Magickal Activity
Creation Spell

Items needed: One 8-pointed star printed on green card stock; one green candle inscribed with the symbol for Venus (♀); a vial of rose oil.

Begin by anointing the candle with the rose oil as you chant:

Goddess of creation, Star of love,
Descend to me from far above.
Grant me wisdom, bring me power,
As I invoke your name this hour.

Next, write out your desire on the back of the eight-pointed star. Light the candle, place it on top of the star, visualize your desire, and invoke Ishtar.

Lady of the Morning Star,
Queen of the heavenly sea.
Power of the mighty wind,
And keeper of the mystery.

Lady who guides the mighty Angels,
Mother of selfless devotion.
Enchantress of the mysteries,
Guardian of time and motion.

Lady I now invite thee here,
As the Virgin of pure love.
The one who moves the soul man,
With her splendor from above.

Lady I now invite thee here,
As the Mother of sacred Earth.
Whose power is beyond compare,
So to my dreams give birth.

Allow the candle to burn for four hours, and then extinguish. Carry the star with you or place it in your desk at work. Repeat this spell once a year to ensure creativity.

28 and 29 January
Up-Helly-Aa

Up-Helly-Aa is a centuries-old fire festival held in the Shetland Islands. It is derived from the ancient Yuletide festival celebrating the triumph of the sun over darkness and winter, and it pays tribute to the ancient Viking Gods and Goddesses. The festival began with torch light processions that ignited giant bonfires and culminated with the burning of a replica of a Viking ship. It was believed that the fire would dispel evil spirits from the villagers and their homes. The festivities usually ended with great feasting and dancing until dawn.

Magickal Activity
Personal Cleansing

This simple rite is based on the power of the Nordic rune sol (sun), the nurturing potentials of the north that are believed to banish, and gently destroy the forces of restriction and constraint. This is especially critical during the shift from darkness to light—from the old to the new.

Items needed: The rune sol (pictured), inscribed with red ink or paint on a piece of heavy construction paper or card stock; one fireproof dish with handles to which is added ¼ cup table salt; one cup 150-percent grain alcohol; six drops Frankincense oil.

Place all the necessary items on your altar. Set the rune next to the fire proof dish containing the salt, alcohol, and oil. Light the alcohol mixture. As it burns, visualize it cleansing the mind and body as you chant:

> *Dark forces fade into night,*
> *But not the power of the sun.*
> *All be cleansed with the power of light,*
> *For now a new time has begun.*

As soon as the fire burns out, pick up the rune, kiss it, and then hang it over the main entrance of your home. Each time you pass beneath the rune, its power will strengthen and energize your mind and body.

30 January
Festival of Peace

At this time the festival of *Pax Romana* was celebrated. It was a term that denoted a period of peace within the Roman Empire and was dedicated to Pax—the Goddess of peace in Rome and Athens.

The *Pax Romana* was a very real and powerful sentiment. Rome's greatness stemmed from its ability to maintain peace throughout a world that had never known the cessation of hostilities.

Magickal Activity
Spell for Peace and Harmony

Items needed: One pink candle; a small vial of Lavender oil; a picture of the person(s) you wish to create peace and harmony between.

Anoint the candle with the lavender oil as you say:

> *Let anger and hostility now depart,*
> *As peace and harmony fill the heart.*

Light the pink candle and visualize peace and harmony filling the heart and mind of the person in the picture as you chant six times:

> *Peace and harmony are what you know,*
> *As love and kindness you now show.*

Allow the candle to burn out and put the picture(s) away.

31 January
Feast of Hecate

Hecate is one of the oldest embodiments of the Triple Moon Goddess worshiped today. She holds power over the heavens, the earth, and the underworld, where she is in control of birth, life, and death. Hecate is the giver of visions, magick, and regeneration. Her chief symbol is the crossroads where all paths connect—the past where one has been, the present where one stands, and future where one is headed. In ancient Rome, statues of Hecate were placed at the important crossroads. Those who frequently traveled would make offerings to the Goddess in return for her blessings.

Magickal Activity
Hecate Blessing Rite

Items needed: An altar or a small table covered with a black cloth; one black candle; a glass or chalice filled with red wine; patchouly incense; a plate filled with bread, goat cheese, and smoked fish; the *Wheel of Hecate* symbol (pictured) inscribed with silver ink on black card stock. (The wheel should be the size of a dessert or small dinner plate.)

To begin the rite, light the black candle as you say:

Mistress of Magick,
Great Hecate,
Let your light
Now lead the way.

Set the plate of food on top of the Wheel of Hecate. Hold your hands over the food and ask Hecate to bless it as follows:

> *I summon thee by Witches rune,*
> > *Waxing light and waning moon.*
> *With the turning of the tide,*
> > *All that's past be laid aside.*
> *Threefold Goddess of the night,*
> > *Bless me from the shadows light.*
> *Banish now all trouble and fear,*
> > *Bring me happiness for all the year.*

You will now want to bless the wine by holding your hands over the chalice or glass of wine as you say:

> *Let now the knowledge of the light,*
> > *Bring me wisdom and inner sight.*
> *For all that was, has now passed away,*
> > *That new beginnings shall come my way.*

In honor of Hecate, eat a portion of the food and drink some of the wine. Take a few moments to reflect on the rite, and then extinguish the black candle as you say:

> *O glorious Hecate your are my power,*
> > *Bless me my Lady from this hour.*

To ensure that Hecate will bless you in the coming year, you must now take the remaining food and wine to the nearest crossroads and leave it. Place the food in the center of the crossroads and pour the wine over it. As you do this, ask Hecate to bless you. When you return home, clear the altar, and hang the Wheel of Hecate over your altar or bed.

February

February was named after the Roman Goddess *Juno Februa*, mother of Mars and the patroness of love and passion. In Latin, *februa* means "to purify by sacrifice," and it was the offerings of goats and a dog that began the great Roman festival of Lupercalia. The Celts considered February to be the month of Imbolg, and the festival of Bride or Brighid. In Anglo-Saxon, the name for February was *Solmonath* for "sun month," noting the gradual return of light after the darkness of Winter.

Often referred to as "The Shadow Month," February reflects the stark reality of Winter and conveys the hope of Spring. As Mother Nature restores herself, snowdrops rise up their white-and green-petaled bells to greet the sun. In some traditions, this short and often hostile month is known as the "cleansing tide," that time between Winter and Spring when the face of Nature is washed clean with snow and rain. Magickally, February is an ideal time to focus on spiritual activities, cleansing, and preparation for the coming year.

Magickal Themes for February:

Preparation, cleansing, creativity

Magickal Correspondences:

Colors:	White, pink, rose
Food:	Bread, lamb, milk, cake, sweet wine
Plants:	Snowdrops, violets, witch-hazel, peony
Stones:	Amethyst, fluorite, staurolite
Symbols:	Brighid, cross, heart, candles
Full Moon:	Storm Moon

1 February
Imbolc/Imbolg

*As the lengthening shafts of sunlight pierce the
earth, all growing things put forth shoots,
buds begin to open and flowers bloom in
great variety. The season of Imbolc
encompasses the sprouting period of young
growth when we emerge from the introspection
of winter to the fresh hope of spring.*
—Caitlin Mathews,
The Celtic Book of Days

Imbolc is one of the four great fire festivals or Sabbats of
the Wiccan religion. Customarily celebrated on February 1,
Imbolc is the "feast of the waxing light" and pays homage to
the Celtic Goddess Brighid.

In Celtic myth and legend, Brighid was the daughter of the
Dagada, the All Father or Great God and King of the Tuath De
Danann (a legendary tribe of people who came from the sky).
Brighid was originally a fire and sun Goddess and considered

the embodiment of poetry, inspiration, and divination. It was her association with fire that linked her to the hearth and home, as well as to the art of smithcraft.

In addition to her fire aspect, Brighid was the major fertility Goddess of the Celtic people. It was a common custom to pray and use votive offerings at her sacred wells in the hope of conceiving. Then, during the pregnancy and birthing process, Brighid was again called upon to protect both mother and child.

Imbolc literally means "in the belly" and signifies the quickening and excitement of the stirring of new life. It was, and still is, the time of the first flowing of the ewe's milk, as they give birth to the lambs. The snow and ice begin to melt. As all of Nature reawakens, now is the time to actively set goals for the coming year. (See Appendix A for Imbolg ritual.)

Magickal Activities
The Candle Wreath

Items needed: Heavy cardboard; eight white candles; eight small candleholders; florist wire; fresh or artificial greenery; tape and glue; pink and white ribbon.

Trace a circle 10 inches wide on the cardboard. Inside the circle, trace a smaller circle about five inches wide. Cut out both circles to form the base for your wreath. Evenly space the candleholders around the cardboard form and glue in place. Wrap the greenery around the cardboard and candleholders to form a wreath. Use florist wire or tape to hold your greenery in place. Wind the ribbon around the wreath, and tie it off with a big bow to one side.

The candle wreath is traditionally placed on a table and used during the Imbolc ceremony. Participants are invited to come forward, light a candle, and make a wish for the coming year.

The Bride Doll

Items needed:　Wheat stalks; string; white linen fabric to make a dress from; glue or tape; a small foam ball.

Begin by wrapping the sheaves of wheat around the foam ball and securing with a piece of string. Just below the tied-off section, twist and glue several stalks to form the arms. Dress

the finished doll in white cotton or linen fabric and place it in a basket.

During the Imbolc ceremony, the bride doll is placed on an altar and blessed by the presiding priesthood. At the conclusion of the ceremony, the doll is taken off the altar and placed next to the front door of the home. It will remain there throughout the night. This is done to honor the Goddess

Brighid, so that she will bless the household with good fortune and fertility for the coming year.

A Prayer for Brighid

Items needed:　One white or pink candle; a vial of rose oil.

Anoint the candle with the oil. As you light it, make your wish and then say the prayer:

> *My Lady Brighid, Goddess of fire,*
> *　　Bless my intentions and grant my desire.*
> *From Summer's sunshine through Winter's snow,*
> *　　You kindle the spark and make hearts glow.*
> *O Gracious Goddess I now ask of thee,*
> *　　To grant to me power, love, and purity.*

2 February
Candlemas (Christian)

St. Mary's Feast of the Candles is officially the feast of the purification and the presentation of Christ in the Temple. In accordance with Mosaic law, Mary came to the Temple 40 days after bearing Jesus both to be purified and to present him, as a male firstborn, to the Lord. It was in the Temple that she met Simeon, who prophesied that Jesus would be "a light unto the world."

In the United States and Canada, February 2 is Groundhog Day. This annual celebration stems from a German belief about a badger that has been transferred to a woodchuck or groundhog. On Candlemas, he breaks his hibernation in order to observe the weather; if he can see his shadow, he returns to his slumbers for six weeks; but if it rains, he stays up and about, because Winter will soon be over.

> *If Candlemas day be fair and bright,*
> *Winter will have another flight.*
> *If Candlemas day be shower and rain,*
> *Winter is gone, and will not come again.*

3 February
St. Blaise's Day or Blaze Day

St. Blaise is considered to be one of the Fourteen Holy Helpers, a group of saints venerated for the supposed efficacy of their prayers for human necessities. He was a Bishop of Sebaste in Armenia who, on his way to execution, miraculously cured a boy who had a fishbone lodged in his throat. He was  thus invoked against throat ailments. An old Armenian folk custom explains that if one ties a knot (pictured) in a cord while asking for St. Blaise's blessing, he or she will be protected from throat ailments.

4 February
King of Frost Day

Prior to World War I, a fair was held on this day in London to honor the *King of Frost*. All the townspeople would gather on the Thames River, normally frozen over at this time, and petition the King of Frost to bring forth Spring. The festival died out during the war.

Along the Welsh border people continue to celebrate this day by gathering snowdrops, sometimes called Candlemas Bells. These tiny bright flowers are tied into bundles and used to purify the hearth and home.

Magickal Activity
Spring House Blessing

To encourage the return of Spring, tie a bunch of snowdrops with green ribbon and hang over the main entrance of your home as you repeat:

> *Candlemas Bells, snowdrops so white,*
> *Cast away shadows, bring forth the light.*

5 February
Fortuna and Saint Agatha's Day

St. Agatha was a Christianized aspect of the Greek Goddess *Tyche*, known to the Romans as *Fortuna* and to the Anglo-Saxons as *Wyrd*. It was the custom to set this day aside for the reading of omens and divining the future, especially by those desiring marriage.

Magickal Activity
Crystal-Gazing

Items needed: A bowl of water; one small clear-quartz crystal; one white candle.

Place the crystal in the bottom of the glass bowl and cover it with water. Place the candle just behind the bowl and light it. With your right index finger, slowly stir the water around the crystal as you chant:

> *Blessed spirits of the night,*
> > *Bless me now with second sight.*

Gaze into the bowl. The water will begin to cloud over, and a psychic mist will appear. When the mist begins to flow out of the bowl, stop stirring the water and look directly into the bowl. Focus your attention on the crystal and repeat the following:

> *Fire and water, crystal clear*
> > *Let the visions now appear.*

Visions of the future will begin to appear. When the visions begin to fade, make a mental note of what you saw. Snuff out the candle and place the crystal under your pillow. The crystal will provide you with more information during your dream time. Later, write your visions down in your diary or dream journal.

6 and 7 February
Li Ch'un, Chinese Festival of Spring

Li Ch'un means "to welcome back the Spring." This annual Spring fertility festival is still celebrated in China. Bamboo and paper effigies of a water buffalo are carried through the streets to the local temple. Upon reaching the temple, the effigies are set on fire and prayers of the people are carried to heaven on the smoke.

Magickal Activity
Wishing Incense

Items needed:

2 Tbs. frankincense   1 tsp. ground cinnamon
1 tsp. ground clove   6 drops orange oil

Mix the ingredients together, and place in an airtight container.

To use the incense, light a church charcoal. When it glows red, sprinkle the incense over the coal. Focus on your desire, and speak your wish into the rising smoke. This can be particularly potent when used by a group of people or an entire family all wishing for the same thing.

8 February
Mass for Broken Needles

In Japan, the art of needlecraft is held in such high regard that all broken needles are brought to the Buddhist temples on this day and honored along with a variety of sewing objects. In rural areas, the Goddess Wakahiru, who oversees weaving, is honored. It is believed that she will provide and make prosperous those she favors.

9 and 10 February
Festival of Yemanjá (Iemanjá of Brazil)

In Afro-Brazilian spiritual traditions, Yemanjá is the Goddess of all sea waters and a symbol of mastery. Her name means "the mother whose children are the fish." She is considered to be a Mother Goddess and has dominion over all large bodies of water, including the depths of the ocean.

Yemanjá is the patron of motherhood and is often associated with the moon. Her colors are blue and white. Her symbols include the fan, mermaid, a silver crescent, and all things that come from the sea.

On this day in Brazil, great festivals honor Yemanjá. They begin at daybreak with ocean-bound processions of singers and dancers, all expressing their love for the Goddess. Those participating carry candles and offerings carved with fish to the sea shore. Thousands of candles in tiny paper boats are set afloat on the ocean as participants make wishes for the coming year.

Magickal Activity
Yemanjá's Magick Wishing Bowl

Items needed: White paper; a white enamel bowl; a blue 7-day candle; seven white fresh chrysanthemum flowers; some blue food coloring or anil (a blueing agent).

Begin by writing your desire on the piece of white paper. Place the paper into the bottom of a white enamel bowl. Set the candle on top of the paper in the bowl, fill the bowl with water, and use the food coloring or anil to color it blue. Carefully place each chrysanthemum flower in the bowl of water, light the candle, and make your wish.

The candle must be left to burn out completely. This will take approximately seven days. At the end of this time, you must take the entire bowl (candle and all) to the nearest large body of water. Gently put the entire contents into the water along with seven silver coins. Make your wish, turn, and walk away. Do not look back.

11 February
Miracle at Lourdes (France)

It was on this day in 1858 that the famous apparition of *Our Lady at Lourdes* was seen by a poor peasant girl, Bernadatte. This was the last manifestation at the gorto, which had been known for many centuries as the shrine of the Goddess.

Born Marie Bernarde Soubrious, Bernadatte (1844–1879) suffered from asthma, poverty, and a lack of education. At the age of 14, on February 11, Bernadatte experienced a vision of the Virgin Mary while collecting firewood on the bank of the River Gave near Lourdes. During the next six months, she saw a series of 18 visions in which the Lady identified herself as "the Immaculate Conception" and told Bernadatte to drink from a nearby spring. The Lady also instructed Bernadatte to erect a chapel on the site. Since that time, the spring has produced 27,000 gallons of water each week and has been the site of countless miracles of healing.

Magickal Activity
Healing Bath

Items needed: One white candle; fresh mint and lavender.

Light the candle and place it next to the tub so the water will reflect its light. As you fill the tub with water, add the mint and lavender leaves. Just before you step into the tub, stir the water with your hand as you chant:

> *Elements and herbs lend your power,*
> *Bring me healing from this hour.*

Soak in the tub for a 15 minutes. At the end of this time, stand up in the tub and let the water out. As the water drains from the tub, visualize all your ailments (or problems) leaving your body and flowing away with the water.

12 February
Holy Day of Diana

Diana was the Roman Goddess of the moon. She was the patroness of hunters and the guardian of the forest, where her

sacred grove stood near Aricia. Diana is called upon to protect animals, children, and the forest. As light and life return
to the earth, her powers of protection are invoked for all creatures great and small.

A Prayer to Diana
Goddess of the hunt, lady of the bow,
I ask you now the way to show.
I pray you bless me from this hour,
With your strength and with your power.
Through times of sorrow and times strife,
Help me make the most of life.

13 February
Parentalia

The ancient Roman festival of *Parentalia* began with the
senior Vestal Virgin performing rites in honor of the dead.
For the following eight days of the festival, each family in Rome
would pay tribute to its ancestors by leaving offerings and gifts
at their graves. During this time, temples were closed, marriages were forbidden, and magistrates did not wear official
insignia.

On the last day of Parentalia a public ceremony was held,
culminating in a sacrifice to Faunus, also known as Pan, a
pastoral and oracular God who revealed the future through
dreams.

Magickal Activity
Dream Magick

Dreams are considered to be the mirror of the soul and a way to divine the future. In some cultures, dreams are considered to be visions of the past or what will come to pass in the future. Many people use dreams as a way to work out personal problems and as an aid in spiritual development.

The Dream Pillow

Items needed: One 10" x 10" square of soft fabric; one cup of mugwort; one cup of chamomile; one cup of mint.

Fold the cloth in half and stitch three of the four sides together to form a case. Fill the case with the herbs and stitch the open side closed. Place the herbal pillow inside your pillow case. Before you retire, reflect on the day's events and then ask Faunus (in your own words) to bring you visions of the future.

14 February
St. Valentine's Day

St. Valentine's Day is a festival of love that amalgamates the Pagan traditions of Rome and northern Europe. Valentine's Day has it origins in the Roman festival of Lupercalia (15 February) honoring Juno and Pan. During this time, unwed women obtained lovers by a form of lottery.

One myth recounts how a bishop named Valentine had conducted weddings for Roman soldiers against an order of

Claudius II forbidding them to marry. When he was condemned to death, he cured the judge's daughter of blindness, and then sent her a letter signed, *your Valentine*.

Magickal Activity

A Love Box

Items needed: A small heart-shaped box painted pink; love-drawing oil; one pink votive candle; a small square of parchment paper; a lock of your own hair; red ribbon; one rose quartz.

Begin by drawing a heart in the center of the parchment paper. Inside the heart inscribe your name and the name of the one you desire or love. Wrap the parchment paper around the lock of your hair and secure it with the red ribbon. Place the parchment, along with the rose quartz, inside the box and close the lid.

Using a pin or sharp object inscribe your name and the name of the one you desire (or love) into the pink candle. Pick up the candle and anoint it with the love-drawing oil as you chant:

> *May the God of love hear my plea,*
> *And bring everlasting love to me.*

Set the candle on top of the box and light it. Gaze into the flame of the candle and visualize the one you love loving you in return. Chant the following seven times:

> *Hail to thee, great God of love,*
> *Shine down on me from far above.*
> *Bring the one I desire to me,*
> *That we shall ever love. So mote it be.*

Just before the candle burns out, drip some of the wax around the lid of the box to seal it shut. On Valentine's Day, present the box to the one you desire as a token of your love and friendship.

15 February
Lupercalia

The Lupercalia was an ancient Roman fertility and purification festival. People assembled at the cave, called the
Lupercal, on the Palantine Hill where Romulus and Remus
were suckled by their wolf foster-mother. Goats and a dog were
sacrificed and young men had their heads smeared with the
blood of the victims, then washed it off with milk, as a death
and rebirth symbol. The youths were naked except for the animal skins, from which thongs were also made and used to strike
women rushing around through the streets. The women put
themselves in the way to receive this fertility magick.

Magickal Activity
Full-Moon Fertility Spell

On the night of the full moon, procure an acorn from the
largest oak tree you can find. Place the acorn in a red pouch,
and carry it with you for one lunar cycle. At the end of the cycle,
return to the oak tree. Facing East, walk three times around
the tree, in a clockwise direction, while you chant with great
force and energy:

> *From seed to tree,*
> > *From tree to me.*
> *From me to thee,*
> > *So mote it be.*

As soon as you have completed the chant, bury the acorn in
the ground next to the tree. Ask a silent prayer for the seed of
a child to grow in your womb, just as the seed of the mighty oak

grows in the ground. When you have finished, leave some money or food in appreciation. Turn, and walk away. Do not look back. You should become pregnant by the next lunar cycle.

16 February
Celebration of Victoria

Victory, called Victoria by the Romans and Nice (Nike) by the Greeks, was a Goddess who was the personification of success or victory. According to her legend she was the daughter of Pallas and Styx and became the patroness of heroes, guiding them to greatness. Revered by the Roman people, she was given an altar in the Senate. This sacred monument became one of the most important symbols of organized Paganism in the Roman Empire and a point of bitter confrontation between the pagans and the Christians in the fourth century A.D. when it was ordered destroyed. The altar was finally abolished in 394 by Theododius I.

17 February
Quirinalia and The Feast of Fools

Quirinalia was a first fruits festival that honored Quirinus, the name given by the Romans to the deified Romulus. As a divinity, Quirinus ranked as one of Rome's most important patrons, along with Mars, Jupiter, and Juno.

Early Rome was divided into 30 *curiae*, each of which had its own day in February for the performing of the Fornacalia, or first-fruits offering to Ceres of toasted emmer-wheat. As the city expanded, the *curiae* were displaced by the new divisions known as *tribus*. As a result, many people did not know which curiae they belonged to. Because of the confusion they were allowed to make the sacrifice on the Quirinalia, which came to be called *The Feast of Fools*.

18 February
Spenta Armaiti
(Persia, festival of women)

The Persian Pagan festival of women known as the Spenta Armaiti was held annually on this throughout all of Persia. During the festival, fertility rites were performed by temple priestesses to honor the Goddess Spandaramet, as well as the Goddess within all women.

Spandaramet was an earth-Goddess whose name comes from the Iranian *spenta aemaita*. She is the Goddess of those who are asleep (the dead). With the coming of Christianity, the word *Spandaramet* took on the meaning of hell.

19 and 20 February
Mesrop Ma tots

This day celebrates the birth of *Mesrop Ma tots*, a missionary to the remoter parts of his native Armenia who, in order to provide his countrymen with books in their own language, invented a 36-letter alphabet (still used today with the addition of a few extra letters). He is also credited with inventing the 38-letter Georgian alphabet.

21 February
Feralia

Feralia is the last day of *Parantalia,* the public festival of the dead. At this time, offerings of food were carried to tombs by each household for use by the dead. This was the equivalent to All Souls' Day.

It was the custom for an ugly old woman, seated amongst girls, to perform magick rituals to appease the Silent Goddess, Tacita. Some rites included placing incense in the mouse holes; casting spells over thread that was then tied to pieces of lead; and placing fish heads sealed with pitch and pierced with pins, into the ground. The latter was done to stop the wagging of the tongue so they could not utter curses.

Magickal Activity
Protection Against Gossip

Items needed: One black candle; a lock of your own hair; an envelope; red sealing wax; a seal with your initial on it; a red marking pen.

Place all the items on a small table or altar. Draw a circle on the outside of the envelope. In the center of the circle, draw a pair of closed lips. Drip some of the sealing wax on the lips and draw an X through them. Place the hair inside the envelope. Light the candle and set it on top of the envelope. Visualize the person who is gossiping about you stopping immediately. As you do this, chant the following:

> *Sealed within I shall be,*
> > *That no harm will come to me.*
> *Your cruel words bounce off me,*
> > *And are now returned back to thee.*
> *For this I now will,*
> > *So mote it be.*

Allow candle to burn out. Bury the envelope.

22 February
Caristia or Cara Cognatio

This was not an official Roman holiday but was nevertheless celebrated on an annual basis. This was a cheerful time that followed the somber activities of the Feralia. Caristia was set aside to renew family ties and settle disputes. There would be a family meal and offerings would be made to the household *Lares*. The holiday was converted into the feast of St. Peter and continued to be celebrated well into the 12th century.

23 February
Terminalia, Shrove-Tide

The Terminalia was an annual ritual held on February 23 to worship Terminus (God of boundary stones or markers) in the temple of Jupiter on Capitoline Hill in Rome. In the country-side, all boundary stones of converging farmers fields were draped with flower garlands, and a sacrifice of blood, wine, and honeycombs was offered to Terminus. A feast followed, attended by all those participating in the rites and their families.

Magickal Activity
Honey Cake

2½ cups flour

1 tsp. allspice

¼ tsp. nutmeg

2 Tbs. cooking oil

Confectioners' sugar

½ tsp. baking soda

¾ tsp. cinnamon

4 eggs, beaten

1 cup honey

Preheat the oven to 350 degrees. Grease and flour a 9" x 13" cake pan. Combine all of the ingredients in a mixing bowl. Pour batter into the pan and bake for 45 minutes. Allow the cake to cool and dust with confectioners' sugar.

24 February
Festival of Shiva

Shiva, the moon God of the mountains, is honored annually on this date. Folklore and myth portray Shiva with the moon in his hair, through which flows the River Ganges. As it poured down from the heavens, Shiva protected the earth against the mighty Goddess Ganga, who could have flooded all of India. Shiva forced her to stream through his matted hair, thus slowing her force until the waters reached the earth. This is why there are so many small streams converging in the lower Himalayas to form one great divine river, the Ganges. It is still believed that her power is so strong that all people, the living as well as the dead, are purified by her holy waters.

During the festival of Shiva, worshipers gather in his temple to celebrate his celestial dance of creation. The sacred rites are followed by an oil lamp vigil known as the Shibaratri (Shiva's night) that culminates with a great feast.

Magickal Activity
Holy Moon Water

Items needed: One glass bowl; silver paint; pure spring water; one round silver floating candle.

Use the silver paint to inscribe a full moon (pictured) on the outside bottom of the bowl.

Place the bowl on a table so the light of the full moon will shine directly on it.

Fill the bowl with the spring water. Float the silver candle on the water and light it as you say:

> *Blessed shall be this sacred fluid,*
> *A gift from the river and sea.*
> *Now made pure by your light,*
> *To bring forth peace and harmony.*

Leave the candle to burn out. Just before sunrise, remove the candle and pour the contents of the bowl into a bottle with a lid, and close tightly. Use the holy moon water in rituals or to bless candles for magickal works.

25 February
Tá Anith Esther

Held in Israel, Tá Anith Esther commemorates Esther's strength when she pleaded with King Ahasuerus to save her people held captive in Persia. It is a quiet time of prayer and reflection that celebrates the feminine nature and those qualities of strength and compassion.

Magickal Activity
Goddess Meditation
Light a blue candle and speak the prayer.

> *How silently, how silently,*
> *The brilliant gift is given.*
> *As the Goddess imparts to human hearts,*
> *Her blessings from her heaven.*
> *No ear may hear her coming,*

> *But in a world often grim,*
> *Where all receiver her still,*
> *The Goddess enters in.*

Relax and meditate on the qualities of compassion and strength.

26 February
Shrove-Tide

Shrove-Tide, first observed in the Middle Ages, was a time of festivity and carnival before Lent started. It was also a festival of the expulsion of Winter, demonstrated by the burning or drowning of an effigy of Winter. Shrove Tuesday, the day before Lent commences on Ash Wednesday, takes its name from being a day of confession of sins—"shrive" or confess. It was the last chance for good food and unrestricted fun before the long period of austerity began. Shrove-Tide became second only to Christmas for it frivolity and "Great Gluttony."

The three days were generally known as Shrove Sunday, Collop Monday, and Shrove Tuesday. Collop Monday takes its name from the habit of eating collops (cuts of fried meat). It only made sense to get rid of all the meat in the house, because it would be banned after Ash Wednesday. Similarly, on Shrove Tuesday, all other perishable foodstuffs were used up.

In Catholic countries, especially France, Shrove-Tide became Fat Tuesday (commonly known as Mardi Gras). This was a time of carnival, with masquerades, singing, and dancing. The festival still continues and has been carried over into America, in particular, New Orleans, Louisiana.

27 February
Equirria

The Equirria was an ancient Roman festival of horse-racing held in honor of the God Mars. It was said to have been established by Romulus and held in the Campus Martius on Caelian Hill. There was a similar festival held on March 14 called the Mamuralia.

Mars was originally a God of agriculture and guardian of fields and boundaries, known as Mamers, Maris, or Marmar. He became identified with the Greek God Ares and so assumed the major role of war God. He was regarded as the son of Juno, and the month of March was named after him. He had a succession of festivals in February, March, and October.

Magickal Activity
The First Pentacle of Mars

The First Pentacle of Mars is used to invoke the powers of Mars for gaining courage, enthusiasm, ambition, and all physical accomplishments.

Items needed: A square of red card stock; one red votive candle in a glass holder; a small red cloth bag.

Inscribe the First Pentacle of Mars (pictured) on the red square of card stock. Light the red votive candle, and place it on top of the pentacle as you chant:

Almighty warrior and God of power,
Fill me with courage from this hour.

Allow the candle to burn completely out. Place the pentacle in the red bag and carry for courage.

28 February
Kalevala Day

The Kalevala is a poetic folk tale of 22,000 verses. It amalgamates folklore with legend, history, and symbolism regarding the Finnish people and their land. The poem was memorized and passed down orally by Finnish bards. In 1836 the poem was finally written down, and this day marks the first day it appeared in print. The Finnish celebrate this day by reading the Kalevala, and then partake of a great feast followed by song, dancing, and drink.

29 February
Leap Year's Day, Job's Birthday

February 29 occurs only once every four years, its addition being designed to rectify the discrepancy between the calendar year of 365 days and the solar year of approximately 365¼ days.

Leap Year is regarded as generally unlucky in Scotland, and Leap Year's Day is especially considered ill-omened; this is because it was Job's birthday, and supposedly the prophet cursed the day he was born. However, the Lord took mercy upon him and thus only allowed it to occur once every four years.

This day is said to be hazardous for men, as ladies have full and absolute license to propose marriage to single gentlemen. Should the gentleman rudely refuse the offer, then he is honor bound to give the lady a present of fresh flowers, white gloves, and chocolate.

March

From the Latin *Martius*, March was originally the first month of the Roman year and derives its name from its chief God of war, Mars. In the Celtic calendar, March (*Martia*) was considered to be the second month of Spring that revolved around the Vernal Equinox. In Wales, this time marked the end of the *amser gwylad* (*ahm-sair-goo-uh-lahd*), the indoor period of Winter that began at the Autumn Equinox. And the Old English name for March was *Hiyd Monath* (the Stormy Month), relating to the fierce winds and inconsistant weather that prevailed at the time.

March officially heralds the season of Nature's rebirth, as darkness gives way to the light after the Winter months. It is a time of promise—of longer and warmer days. March is traditionally a month of varied weather, foreshadowed by the saying, "March comes in like a lion and goes out like a lamb" or occasionally the other way around. March is an ideal time to clear away mental and emotional debris and to plant the seeds of desire that will bring about a bountiful harvest.

Magickal Themes for March:
Planning, ploughing, planting

Magickal Correspondences:

Colors:	Lavender, pink, yellow
Food:	Eggs, spinach, fish, figs, almond cake
Plants:	Dandelion, periwinkle, dill, violet
Stones:	Sugilite, beryl, blue topaz
Symbols:	Mars, egg, basket, fish,
Full Moon:	Chaste Moon

1 March
Roman New Year, Kalends of March, Matronalia

Let us not look back in anger, or forward in fear,
but around in awareness.
—James Thurber

The *Kalends,* or first day of the month, was sacred to Juno, especially the first day of the month of March. This was originally the beginning of the Roman year, still marked in classical times by the tending of the sacred fire of the Goddess Vesta and the affixing of fresh laurels to the Regia (the home of the *pontifex maximus*).

The first day of March also marked the *Matronalia*, a festival held in honor of women, and the founding of the temple of *Juno Lucina*. In the home, prayers were offered for prosperous wedlock, and the women of the household received presents from the men. In addition, all female slaves were given the day off and the head of the house would wait on them.

Magickal Activity
Love Attraction Spell

Items Needed: One gold candle; small square of parchment
paper; red ink pen.

Place the candle and paper on a small table. Take several
deep breaths and relax. Use the red pen to write a description
of the person you want to attract on the parchment paper. Light
the candle and visualize your dream lover. When the crown of
the candle begins to fill with wax, fold the paper into a small
packet and seal it shut with wax from the candle as you chant:

> *O golden tear drop in a wax sea,*
> *As the flame drifts skyward,*
> *Bring my love to me!*

Allow the candle to burn out, and carry the packet in your
purse or briefcase.

2 March
St. Chad and the Holy Wells Day

This day was sacred to St. Chad, in Old English Cheadda,
pronounced Chad-da, the patron saint of healing wells and
medicinal springs; St. Chad would spend hours in meditation
and prayer, naked and immersed in water up to his neck. His
symbol was the *Crann Bethadh*, the tree of life.

The tradition on this day is to make an offering of flowers
and sweet cakes to the deity of the well or spring closest to your
home. For those who dwell in the city, place a small table with
a fountain on it near the front door. Place your flowers and

cakes next to the fountain. Ask a simple blessing for good fortune for the coming year. When you enter your home, drop a coin in the fountain for continued prosperity.

3 March
Hina Matsuri (Dolls' Festival)

Dolls' Day, or *Hina Matsuri*, is a very symbolic holiday in which young Japanese-American girls receive new dolls and display their doll collections. The holiday is sometimes called the Peach Festival, because it is the custom to adorn the dolls with peach blossoms—the symbol of peace and mildness.

In Japanese homes, the dolls are placed on a five-step shelf. The two principle or most regal of the dolls are placed at the top and those of lesser quality or rank are placed on the lower shelves. The dolls serve as models of decorum; their calm, smiling faces and neat appearance are exemplary of the gentility and refinement that are expected from the young girls of the household.

The dolls are kept exhibited for several days, and the festival provides occasions for family reunions and visits to admire often elaborate displays. In honor of the dolls, hot tea, diamond-shaped rice cakes, sweet wine, candies, and cookies are offered to the dolls and their visitors. At some point during the festivities, girls receive lovely additions to their collections from their parents, relatives, and friends.

4 March
Feast of Rhiannon

It is a popular custom for the Wiccans of Wales and Ireland to honor the Goddess Rhiannon this day. Known as "Rigantona," meaning *Great Queen*, Rhiannon has been identified with the popular Gaulish mare Goddess *Epopna*.

Rhiannon's divine status is indicated by her first encounter with Pwyll, the king of Dyfed. Riding slowly past him on a large white horse, he was entranced and pursued her. But even with the swiftest of mounts he could not overtake her. Finally, in desperation, he called out to her. Rhiannon stopped to converse with him, admitting she was seeking him out. Pwyll won Rhiannon's love and when she arrived at his court to be married, she brought precious gifts for all the nobles. Thus her image of a generous, bountiful queen-Goddess.

Magickal Activity
Apple on a String (Love Spell)

Select a large red apple. Mark sections on the outside peel by scraping lines into the skin. Into each one of the sections, scrape the name or initials of the persons that you wish for lovers.

Tie a string to the stem of the apple and hang it from any support. Next, twirl the apple around so that when you release it, it will spin in a clockwise direction. Hold a 3-inch needle in your hand and as the apple begins to twirl, close your eyes, and repeat the following chant:

> *Bountiful Queen, Goddess of love,*
> > *Shower your blessings from above.*
> *As I work this apple spell,*
> > *Show me the one who will love me well.*

As you finish the chant, push the needle all the way into the apple, steadying the fruit with your other hand. The name in the section were the pin has pierced will be your true lover.

5 March

Navigium Isidis
(The Festival of the Ship of Isis)

The ancient festival of *Navigium Isidis* celebrated the Goddess Isis's invention of the sail and her patronage of sailing that began each new sailing season.

Isis Euploia—Isis of Good Sailing—sailed with the crew of Ra on their journey through the underworld searching for the severed parts of her murdered husband Osiris. As the beloved Goddess of Alexandria, whose massive lighthouse guided ships far at sea to shore, Isis was invoked to protect all incoming as well as outgoing vessels. Akin to *Yemanjá* (February 9–10), Isis was worshiped at the shore and on the sea. She was considered the guardian of the grain ships that brought the bounty of Egypt to Rome. As her worship took root along the trade routes, seafarers would leave offerings and petition her protection before embarking on treacherous journeys.

Magickal Activity

Protection Amulet

Items needed: 5" x 7" piece of blue cloth; dark green fabric paint or marker; one lapis-lazuli stone; one lotus pod; ½ tsp each of lavender, jasmine, rosemary.

On the piece of cloth, inscribe the *Eye of Horus* (often painted on ships for protection) with the fabric paint. Fold the cloth in half (bottom to top) and sew the sides together, leaving the top open.

Begin by focusing on your goal. In your own words, ask the Goddess for her blessing. Place the lapis and herbs into the pouch as you chant:

> *Goddess of the starry sea,*
> > *Lord of the watchful eye.*
> *Let no harm come to me,*
> > *Or those that may pass me by.*
> *Protect me as I go my way,*
> > *With your powers from above.*
> *Be it night or be it day,*
> > *Bless me with your perfect love.*

Allow yourself several minutes to reflect on the Goddess Isis and her protective qualities. Sew the top of the pouch shut and carry when you travel. Or, give the pouch as a gift to a friend who is planning a trip.

6 March
Whale Festival

During the first week of March, people who live along the Northern most part of California take time to visit the shore. This is a time of great anticipation and excitement as everyone hopes to catch a glimpse of the annual whale migration—a deeply moving and inspiring event.

One of the three royal fish of ancient Britain, whales are considered record-keepers and symbols of regeneration. The idea of being swallowed by a whale is equivalent to the initiation process of death and rebirth, the whale being both tomb and womb simulatenously. The Norse believed that Witches could ride whales, and in Japan the whale is the sea mount for the God of oceans.

7 March
Nones of March/Junonalia/Phra Buddha Bat Fair

In ancient Rome, Nones (in Latin, "Nonae") were the nine days before the Ides (the 7th in long months and the 5th in other months) when the holidays for the month were announced. *Junonalia* honored the Goddess Juno with a procession of 27 girls, dressed in long flowing robes, accompanied by an image of the Goddess carved from the wood of a cypress tree.

On this day in Thailand, the annul bat fair is held in honor of the Buddha's footprint. The festival features folk dancing and traditional handcrafts. Local shrines and statues are honored with food, flowers, and personal offerings of thread and yarn.

8 March
Mother Earth Day

On this day in China, the Goddess Hu Tu is honored as Mother Earth with parades, fireworks, and feasting. Offerings of flowers, coins, and incense are placed in small holes in the ground, blessed, and then covered with soil to bring prosperity and good fortune to the community. Dating back to the Sung dynasty, the celebration pays homage to the ground itself in the form of the great Goddess of productivity, fertility, and the elements of wind and rain. In many ways this commemoration of the earth resembles our own Earth Day that honors the spirit of Gaia.

Magickal Activity
Gaia Offering

Items needed: One green votive candle and holder; fresh flowers; patchouli incense.

Place all the required items on a table or altar covered with a green cloth. Light the incense. Take a few moments to meditate on the Goddess Gaia, your connection to her, and the earth. In your own words, ask the Goddess to bless and protect you and your family. Light the candle and place it in front of the flowers as you recite the blessing:

> *To your heavenly vault I lift my eyes,*
> *My hopes fears at your feet are laid.*
> *For you who built the earth and skies,*
> *Shall keep me strong and unafraid.*

Leave the candle to burn out. Place the flowers in the main room of your home as a reminder of the power and potential of the Goddess.

9 March
Butter Festival

The annual Butter Festival, held on this day in Tibet by the Buddhist monks, illustrates their belief that the world is transient—that only the spirit is eternal. Preparing for this festival takes months of time consuming work as dye is mixed with iced butter to create the effigies, some of which are two stories high.

When the day of the festival arrives, the statues are mounted on platforms with lanterns. Near dusk the statues are paraded through the streets as sacred chants are recited. After the procession the statues are taken to the river and tossed upon the water to melt away.

10 and 11 March
Herakles/Hercules

This day celebrates the super-human strength of the Greek hero-God Herakles, son of Alcmene by Zeus. His many adventures included fighting a bull-headed snake to win the love of his earthly wife Deianeira. During the battle, he tore off one of the animal's horns, which became the cornucopia. He then fought and killed the centaur Nessus, who had tried to rape her. Before Nessus died, he gave Deianeria some of his blood to put on Herakles's tunic as a charm to keep his love. But the blood poisoned Herakles by burning him. Distressed, Herakles sacrificed himself upon Mt. Oeta. When Herakles was admitted to Mt. Olympus as a God, Zeus gave him his daughter Hebe for his wife. They had two children, Alexiares and Anicerus.

12 March
Babylonian Feast of Marduk

From as early as the Third Dynasty of Ur, Marduk was venerated as the God of the city of Babylon. He was so popular that his worship spread through Assyria from about the 14th century B.C. The worship of Marduk even in its most extreme form could be compared with monotheism, but it never led to the denial of other Gods or to the exclusion of female deities.

13 March
Feast of Purification

This date marks the Balinese feast of purification, the time of the year when the lord of hell cleans out his underworld lair and all manner of demons and evil spirits are left to roam Bali free. During this time—when evil is afoot—the natives go to elaborate ends to purify both their individual homes as well as the island. No corner or stone is left untouched as rites of purification and spells for protection are recounted.

Magickal Activity
Protection Bottle

Items needed: One small jar; enough of the following items to fill the jar: broken glass, nails, thorns, steel wool, wormwood, thistle, nettles, vinegar, salt, your own urine; one black candle; one red felt marker.

Fill a bottle with all the items and seal tightly. On the top of the lid, draw a pentacle with the red felt marker. Place the black candle on the lid of the jar and light it. Chant the following over the candle:

> *Candle of black, and hexes old,*
> > *Release the powers that you hold.*
> *Reverse the flow of spells once cast,*
> > *Leave pain and sorrow in the past.*

Let the candle burn out. Take the bottle and bury it in the earth close to your home. The bottle will protect you and your family from harm. In most cases, the bottle will form a shield of protection for about six months. When the spell begins to weaken, just repeat by making a new bottle.

14 March
Equirria

This is the second *Equirria* festival held in honor of the Roman God Mars (also 27 February). There was a festival of *Mamuralia* also recorded for this date, but it is unclear if this was a separate festival for *Mamurius Veturius*, legendary maker of the sacred shields or just another name for the *Equirria*.

The 14th of March also celebrates the runic half-month of *Beorc*, ruled by the Goddess of the birch tree associated with Frigga. This is a time of symbolic purgation in preparation for the new beginnings of Spring and Summer.

15 March
Buzzard Day

The buzzards (turkey vultures) of Hinckley, Ohio, return like clockwork on this day each year. Their uncanny return to Hinckley Ridge on March 15 has been the subject of folk legends dating back nearly 150 years. It seems that no one paid them much attention until a reporter, in 1957, from the *Cleveland Press* took an interest. When his article about the buzzards appeared in the paper along with the prediction that they would return on exactly March 15, interest in the birds mounted. By the time March 15 arrived in Hinckley, so did the buzzards—right on time. The news traveled fast, bringing media from Ohio, Pennsylvania, and Indiana. The small township of Hinckley was unprepared for the more than 9,000 bird  watchers that ultimately descended upon them. From that day on, the town dedicated March 15 to the *Buzzards of Hinckley*. The town council immediately made plans to deal with the throngs of people that would return every year along with the buzzards. In time, the fame of the Hinckley buzzards spread. Today, their legendary return rivals stories of the "Swallows of Capistrano."

An old manuscript account by William Cogswell, one of the first white men to set foot in the county in 1810, made several references to "vultures of the air" at the gallows of the Big Bend in the Rocky River, where an Indian squaw had been hung for Witchcraft. Then again in December of 1818, there is reference to the "Great Hinckley Varmint Hunt." More than 475 men lined up along Hinckley's 25-square-mile perimeter and began moving inward to rid the area of predatory animals killing livestock. It is believed that the tons of butchered refuse attracted the vultures. No one really knows for sure what the enticement is, but every year on March 15 the buzzards of Hinckley return.

16 March
Festival of Holi

Holi, a Spring holiday, is celebrated on this day by the Hindus. It's a favorite day among children, probably because they get to throw red-colored water on anyone who passes them by. Each village has a central bonfire dedicated to the Krishna, an incarnation of the God Vishnu. The ashes that result from the sacred fire are then rubbed on the people's foreheads to bring them good fortune in the coming year.

17 March
St. Patrick's Day

St. Patrick, born near Severn in Britain around 389 A.D., is the patron saint of Ireland. It is believed that when he was 16 he was stolen from his home by Irish outlaws and then sold as a slave. After six years of slavery, he escaped into Gaul, where he became a Christian. He returned to the land of his captivity as a bishop in the hopes of converting the people to Christianity.

He was highly successful in his work and by his death Ireland was well on its way to becoming a Christian nation. He is most famous for driving all of the snakes from Ireland, although scientists attest there were none there at the time. His name is always associated with the shamrock because he was in the habit of wearing one as a symbol of the Trinity (God the Father, the Son, and the Holy Ghost).

The most notable activities of Saint Patrick's day are the numerous parades that are held in his honor and the drinking of Irish Coffee, which began more than 27 years ago at the Buena Vista Café, not far from the bottom of the Leavenworth Street cable car line in San Francisco.

The Original Irish Coffee
Ingredients (1 serving)

1 cup coffee, freshly brewed   3 sugar cubes
1 jigger Irish Whiskey

Pour the coffee into a large mug. Add sugar and stir to
dissolve. Add whiskey and stir to combine. Top with whipped
cream and serve.

18 March
Sheila-Na-Gig

The Irish Goddess of fertility, known as Sheila-Na-Gig,
was annually honored on this date in ancient times. Many bas-

reliefs of this Goddess figure have been found
on medieval churches, priories, convents, and
some castles. Usually depicted as a squatting
female figure, displaying exaggerated genitals
and yawning vulva, she represents the Great
Mother in her most ambiguous form. The
Sheila-Na-Gig is associated with the genera-
tive principle of Nature. Her image, repro-
duced in amulet form, is worn for protection—possibly from
harm or for safe sex.

19 March
Quintaria/Quinquatrus

In Ancient Greece, the day before the Vernal (Spring) Equinox was dedicated to the Goddess Athena. In Rome this was the fifth day after the Ides of March—the start of the five-day festival for the God Mars and the principal festival of the Goddess Minerva. The first day was her birthday and the following four days were devoted to circus games.

Minerva (pictured) was the Goddess of crafts and trade guilds. She was originally the Etruscan Goddess *Menrva* and identified with the Greek Goddess Athena. In Rome, Minerva had a temple on the *Aventine Hill* and another in the *Forum of Nerva*. Her festivals were held on March 19, June 19, and September 13.

20–22 March
Ostara/Spring or Vernal Equinox

The Equinox is the time when the sun crosses the plane of the equator, making day and night of equal length. This is the actual beginning of Spring and occurs somewhere between the 20th and 22nd of March. In fact, most of our modern-day Easter customs come from the Pagan Ostara, named after the Saxon Goddess Eostre. This is a time of balance, equality, and harmony between the masculine and feminine forces in Nature, the time of year when practitioners of the Wiccan religion, both physically as well as symbolically, plant the seeds of their desires—seeds that in time will grow into plants representing individual, long-term goals, that began at Yule, the Winter Solstice and rebirth of the sun. (See Appendix A for an Ostara Ritual.)

Magickal Activities
Prosperity Seed Spell

Items needed: Marigold seeds; a clay pot filled with earth; one green candle; a small topaz stone; green paint and brush; a small square of paper.

Paint the rune symbol for wealth on the clay pot and on the paper. Put the topaz stone along with the paper in the bottom of the pot, and fill it with the earth. Place the pot and seeds, along with the candle, on a small table or altar covered with a green cloth.

Light the candle. Pick up the seeds and hold them as you mediate on what it is you need. For more than one participant, put the seeds on a small plate so that each person can take a seed and plant it, making his or her own wish. When you feel the time is right, plant the seeds as you chant:

> *Seeds and earth,*
> *To dreams give birth.*

Leave the candle to burn for four hours. Extinguish the candle and place it along with the pot in a window. Each time you water the seeds, light the candle and repeat the chant. This is a great activity for the whole family, particularly if family members have a collective goal in mind.

Spring Wand-Making

Items needed: A small tree branch; three silver coins; three sugar cookies; three each of walnuts, hazel nuts, and almonds; a sharp knife; a paper bag.

Use the chart that follows to choose the wood for the wand you want to make.

Tree Correspondences	
Birch - New Beginnings	Rowan - Magick
Hawthorn - Protection	Oak - Power Magick
Hazel - Wisdom	Apple - Love
Poplar - Success	Pine - Birth
Maple - Longevity	Cedar - Strength
Beech - Divination	Elm - Dignity

Place the coins, cookies, and nuts in the paper bag. Choose the tree from which you want to make your wand. Go to the tree, and in your own words ask for permission to cut one of its small, new branches. Neatly cut the branch from the tree. Thank the tree for its branch. Gently place the coins, cookies, and nuts at the base of the tree as an offering of thanksgiving.

Trim the branch so that it measures from the inside of your elbow to the tip of your middle finger. This measurement makes the wand uniquely yours. Scrape the bark off of the branch and allow the wood to dry. Once the wood is thoroughly dry you will want to carve or paint your own personal symbols on it.

23 March
Summer Finding/Marzenna/Dance of Salii

The Norse festival of Summer Finding celebrates the light of the sun becoming stronger and more powerful than the darkness.

The old Pagan festival of *Marzenna* is still celebrated in the Polish countryside with dancing, singing, and the burning of straw effigies to welcome back the Spring.

In ancient Rome, the priests would invoke the Gods Mars and Saturn by dancing with swords and clashing holy shields. It was believed this display of power and strength would drive the evil spirits of Winter back, thus allowing the new growth of Spring to blossom forth.

24 March
The Day of Heimdall

This day celebrates the horn-sounding guardian God of the Rainbow Bridge to Valhalla who, as Rig, was the progenitor of each of the different classes of traditional society. He was the God of orderliness and has been equated with the archangel Gabriel—lord of the moon and patron of everything that grows upon the earth.

Prayer for the Angel Gabriel to Grant a Wish
In honor of Gabriel, light a violet votive candle and ask for something you need by saying:

> *In the name of the Great Creator of all that is, I call upon Gabriel, guardian of the Moon, and all that grows upon the earth to grant me—*(state wish)—*this special favor that I shall realize—*(repeat wish)—*for the good of myself and to harm none.*

25 March
Hilaria

Hilaria is the ancient Roman festival held in honor of Attis and Cybele. There were many days leading up to this festival when the actual ceremonies took place. This was a day of rejoicing, celebratng the resurrection from Winter to Spring, from darkness to light. The festivities culminated with a *ceremony of washing* that was believed to promote fertility.

26 and 27 March
Liberalia / Smell the Breeze Day

The wine God Liber Pater was annually honored on this day in ancient Rome. His festival was a time of great feasting, dancing, and drinking. It was believed that by participating in the festival, young men entering into manhood would be gifted with strong sons and bountiful crops.

In Egypt, the little-known festival of *Smell the Breeze Day* commemorates the Easter holiday and Spring with festive outings. It is believed that if one smells a fresh-cut onion at dawn he or she will be blessed with good luck and good health.

28 March
The Sacrifice of Tombs/St. Mark's Eve

According to the cosmological text, *De Pascha Computus*, written in 243 A.D., the sun and moon were created on Wednesday, March 28. This was also the date of the nativity of *Jesus of Nazareth* before it was changed by the Catholics at Rome, in 336 A.D., and again by the Orthodox at Constantinople 377 A.D.

March 28 was the date of the old Roman festival of *The Sacrifice of Tombs*, when the departed ancestors were remembered and honored, similar to present-day Catholic services in cemeteries on All Souls' Day. This is also St. Mark's Day, a time of divination, when the other world is a little more accessible than usual.

29 March
Festival of Inanna/Ishtar (New Year in Mesopotamia)

The most significant rite of the new year was the *hieros gamos*—the holy marriage between the king, who represented the God Dumuzi, and one of the temple priestess, who represented the Goddess Inanna. It was ordained that the King of Summer, no matter what his lineage, must become the husband of the life-giving Goddess of love, Inanna of Uruk. The role of the priestess of Inanna was that of the dominant partner who makes love to the king. The ceremony was called the *"fixing of destinies"* and determined the prosperity of the New Year. The entire ritual took place in a chapel on the summit of the ziqqurat and was considered essential for the fertility of the land.

Magickal Activity
The Marriage Charm

Bind two small gold rings together with a white ribbon. Hold the bound rings in both hands as you chant the following over them:

> *With body and spirit*
> *   As these rings entwine*
> *Unite our souls*
> *   Our essence combine.*

Place the rings in your pocket or purse. Carry them with you whenever you are with the one you wish to marry.

30 March
Festival of Janus and Concordia

Janus, the Roman *God of Doorways* and of *The Turn of the Year*, along with Concordia the *Goddess of Peace* and *Civic Harmony,* were honored at this time. Even in the ancient world, March was a time of change—turning from darkness to light—a time of equality, peace, and harmony. In Norse tradition, this day begins the runic half-month *Ehwaz* (the horse month), a time of partnerships between humans and Nature, as represented in the relationship between rider and horse.

31 March
Roman Festival of Luna

On this day the Roman festival of Luna celebrated the Goddess of the full moon whose temple on the Aventine Hill was the focus of worship. As the Goddess of the moon, Luna represents growing awareness, the fulfilment of love, and the mystery of enchantment. She is at once both lover and mother to her suitors and is identified with Diana and Selene.

Magickal Activity

Items needed: One silver candle; one teaspoon ground
allspice; almond oil.

On the night of the waxing moon, inscribe the silver candle with the exact amount of money you need. Rub the candle with the almond oil as you chant the following:

> *As the moon doth wax and grow,*
> *So to me doth money flow.*

Once you feel the candle is thoroughly charged with your wish, roll it in the allspice and light. Allow the candle to burn for one hour and then extinguish. Repeat this spell each night, at the same time, until the moon is full. On the night of the full moon, allow the candle to burn out.

April

The fourth month of the Gregorian calender comes from the Latin *aperire,* meaning "to open." Named for the Greek Goddess Aphrodite (Roman Venus), this second month of Spring is time of expectancy, as the earth opens to receive the seed of life.

The Anglo-Saxons named April *Eastermonth,* in honor of the Goddess Eostre, whose name is the origin of the word *Easter*. The Irish named it Aibrean, and the modern followers of Asatru call it Ostara.

April is a month of warmth and ever-growing light. Trees and plants come to life. The song of migrating birds fills the air as soft gentle rains promote the joy of growth and renewal. April is the time to take action—to physically put effort into those goals inaugurated at the beginning of the year.

Magickal Themes for April:

Plant; take action; journeying

Magickal Correspondences:

Colors:	Green, yellow, purple
Food:	Salmon, pork, oatmeal, wine
Plants:	Woodruff, bluebell, rose, marigold
Stones:	Bloodstone, garnet, ruby
Symbols:	Maypole, crown of flowers cauldron
Full Moon:	Seed Moon

1 April
April Fools' Day

Even if you're on the right track,
you'll get run over if you just sit there.
—Will Rogers

April Fools' Day, the classic Festival of Fools ruled over by the Norse trickster God Loki. In the rural countryside of Scotland this is "hunt the gowk day" (cuckoo—hence fool) and a time to send friends on pointless errands for articles such as pigeons' milk, hens' teeth, and elbow grease.

The origins of the day are uncertain, but it may have originated in France. It was the custom on this day to fool the evil spirits that were believed to be about so that they would not interfere with fertility—a necessity in ancient times.

Another theory is that when the Gregorian calendar moved the New Year from March 25 to January 1 in 1582, those who failed to make the proper adjustments were April fools.

2 and 3 April
Rejoicing Day

In Germany, this is a time of rejoicing with the return of warm weather. In some regions, the old custom of "carrying death away" is still practiced. Straw effigies are carried through the streets and placed on a central bonfire. As the last of the effigies is consumed, Winter succumbs to Spring.

4 April
Megalesia Mater

This day marked the beginning of *Ludi Megalenses*, the first day of the weeklong *Megalesia Mater* in honor of the Goddess Cybele—generally described as Magna Mater. Her cult originated in Asia Minor and came to be centered on Mount Dindymus at Pessinus in Phyrgia, where she was known as Agdistis. Her consort was Attis, and there was a great deal of mythology that surrounded their relationship.

It was during the war with Carthage that Cybele's cult was brought to Rome in 204 B.C., following a prophecy in the *Sibylline Books* and advice from the *Oracle at Delphi*. The prophecy stated that the invaders would be driven back if Magna Mater was brought to Rome. Soon after, her sacred black stone was brought to Rome and housed in the temple of Victoria, later to be placed in a temple on the Palatine Hill, which was dedicated to Magna Mater in 191 B.C.

The Megalesia lasted from April 4 to 10 and originally consisted of games in the Circus Maximus. It was a festival of fertility in the most primal of forums. A large pine tree representing the God Attis was adorned with white cloth and placed in the center of the temple of Cybele. The novice priests would then cut their arms and sacrifice their virility to the God. The severed portions of their manhood were dashed against the pine tree and then buried. This brutal and bloody display of adoration was considered instrumental in recalling Attis to life, and thus the return of summer growth.

Magickal Activity
Crystal Divination

As it was the Oracle of Delphi that brought Cybele to Rome, the act of divining the future became associaed with her. It seems only fitting to celebrate the power of this Goddess by working with some form of divination on this day. For this magickal activity you will need a clear glass bowl filled with spring water, a quartz crystal, and a white taper candle.

Place the crystal in the clear glass bowl and cover it with the spring water. Set the white candle just behind the bowl and light it. With your right index finger, slowly stir the water around the crystal as you chant:

> *Blessed spirits of the night,*
> > *Bless me now with second sight.*

Focus your attention on the water. It will begin to cloud over with a fine mist. Once the mist begins to flow out of the bowl, stop stirring the water and look directly into the bowl. Center your attention on the crystal and repeat the following:

> *Fire and water, crystal clear,*
> > *Let the visions now appear.*

Visions of the future will appear. When the visions begin to fade, make a mental note of what you saw. Snuff out the candle and place your crystal under your pillow. The crystal will provide you with more information during your dream time. Later, write your visions down in your dream journal or magickal Book of Shadows.

5 April
Festival of Kwan Yin

In China and Japan thousands of people share a love for this Goddess of compassion, healing, and mercy. To this day, Kwan Yin is still widely worshipped, and, in general, most Eastern households will have at least one shrine dedicated to her. At the temple of Miao Fend Shan, near Peking, devotees make their annual pilgrimage to her shrine on this day. Many ask for healing and the power to rid them of life's pains and sorrows. As her compassion is invoked, offerings of incense, violet-colored candles, and petitions written on rice paper are placed at her shrines.

Magickal Activity
Kwan Yin Shrine

Items needed: A small table or corner shelf covered with a white cloth; a small white or crystal vase filled with water (to represent Kwan Yin's dew pot); sea shell; one white flower; a bowl of water; one white flower-shaped floating candle; a picture or statue of Kwan Yin; sandalwood joss sticks and holder.

Place the statue at the back of the shelf or table. Set the vase and the incense holder to the right-front of the statue (or picture). Put the floating candle, flower, and sea shell in the bowl. Set this in front of the statue (or picture). In your own words, ask Kwan Yin to bless you and those you love with good health, good fortune, and compassion. Light the floating candle, and recite her benediction:

> Grant me light that I shall know,
>   The wisdom thou alone can give;
> That truth shall guide all that I do,
>   And virtue bless the way I live.
> O grant me light that I shall learn,
>   How empty is life from thee apart.
> But, how sure is joy when I return,
>   To thee with an open heart.

It is appropriate to allow the candle and incense to burn out. You may repeat Kwan Yin's simple ceremony whenever you feel the need for her blessings.

6 and 7 April
Boat Festival/Tater Day

The annual boat festival held in France celebrates the return of springtime. Children make miniature boats with candles in them that symbolize the joy of sailing on the "seas of life." At the end of the day, a great procession ends at the Rhine, where the boats are cast onto the water as everyone makes their wish for the coming Summer months.

Batats (sweet potatoes), brought to the New World by Christopher Columbus, became a dietary staple and one of the primary crops grown in the southern United States, where they are as rampant as the kudzu vine. The small tuber is rich in vitamin A and mainly grown for human consumption in the form of alcohol, flour, and starch.

Originally a market where potato slips for Spring planting were sold, Tater Day has been revived as a country fair. In Benton, Kentucky, Sweet Potato Day comes complete with a beauty pageant, horse races, carnival games, and a flea market. Celebrated since 1843, Tater Day is one of the oldest trade days in the United States.

Sweet Potato Pudding

1 egg	¼ cup melted butter
1⅓ cup milk	¼ tsp. nutmeg
½ cup sugar	1 cup grated sweet potatoes
¼ tsp. allspice	Pinch of salt

Beat egg and add remaining ingredients. Pour into a greased baking dish. Bake at 400 for 30 minutes or until thick, stirring occasionally. Serves 4.

8 April

Hanamatsuri, Birthday of the Buddha

Siddhartha-Gautama-Shaka, commonly called the Buddha, which in Sanskrit means "the enlightened one," was born on this day around 563 B.C. In his youth, Siddhartha lived a life of sheltered luxury. At the age of 29 he left his palace home and for the first time encountered the poverty, suffering, and death of the common people. From that moment forward he dedicated his life to the pursuit of enlightenment. At 35 he achieved enlightenment, becoming a Buddha. For the next 45 years he traveled teaching Buddha's Dharmas—a way of life patterned after his own path of enlightenment.

Among the Buddhist holidays, the celebration of April 8 is the most important. To commemorate his birthday, Buddhist temples in Japan and America alike construct a platform that is covered with flowers. On the platform, an image of the infant Buddha is placed in a tub filled with licorice tea. The members of the temple then take part in pouring licorice tea over the figure of the Buddha to signify the act of bathing him. They will then drink some of the sweet tea themselves, an act that is supposed to effect the purification of their spirits and make them Buddha-like.

Magickal Activity
Prayer of the Bell

For this activity you will need a bell or gong and a prayer mat (a small woven mat used for prayer). Turn down the lights, sit comfortably on the mat, and place the bell or gong in front of you. Take several deep breaths. Relax and speak the prayer.

> *Would that the sound of the bell might go beyond
>   our earth,*
> *And be heard even by all the denizens of the darkness
>   Outside the Iron Mountains.* (ring bell)
> *Would that their organ of hearing becoming pure,
>   beings might attain perfect direction.* (ring bell)
> *So that every one of them might come finally to the
>   Realization of supreme enlightenment.* (ring bell)

9 April
A-Ma or Matzu Festival

On this day in Portugal and China, the Goddess Matzu, patroness of all fishermen and sailors, is honored. Altars are set with offerings of seafood, fresh flowers, and sweets. Parades to the seashore and fireworks are thought to bring the blessings of the Goddess to all whose living depends upon the often turbulent ocean depths.

10 April
Megalesia

In Ancient Rome, this day saw the culmination of the *Megalesia,* with games in the Circus Maximus preceded by a grand procession to the Great Mother's temple on the *Palatium* now called Palatine Hill. This last day was one of great festivity. There were horse and chariot races, games, and a magnificent procession. A silver statue of Cybele, drawn by a garland wagon and escorted by an orchestra of flutes, drums, and symbols, made its way to the tributary of the Tiber River. The statue was then baptized with water by purple-robed priests. Upon its return to the temple, the procession was pelted with fresh spring flowers. Of this majestic site *Ovid* (*Fasti, IV 389*) writes:

> *When the next dawn shall have looked on victorious Rome, and the stars shall have been put to flight and given place to the sun, the Circus will be thronged with a procession and an array of the deities, and the horses, fleet as the wind, will contend for the first palm.*

11 April
Anahita

Anahita, Persian river Goddess and patroness of marriageable girls and childbirth. Also worshiped in Babylon, where on this day the daughters of noble families gave their virginity as her temporary sacred prostitutes.

12–19 April
The Cerealia/Chu-Si-Nu Festival

The Cerealia is an ancient Roman holiday to honor the Goddess of grain, Ceres. The festival began on April 12 and concluded on April 19. As with most of the Spring festivals, the Cerealia was celebrated to secure fertility for the crops. Most of the activities were held inside the Circus Maximus, including the yoking of a bull and a rather bizarre fox chase. Burning brands were tied to the foxes tails and then they were set loose among the people.

In Taiwan, the Goddess Chu-Si-Nu who presides over childbirth is honored at this time. One of the customs is for pregnant women to go the temple of Chu-Si-Nu and ask for her blessing on their unborn children.

13 April
Thailand Water Festival

April 13 marks the annual three-day festival of water celebrated by the Buddhists in Thailand. The temples are cleaned and then purified with the smoke of incense. All of the Buddha statues are then ritually bathed, and the water is thrown on those attending the ceremony to "wash away" the evil spirits of the previous year.

14 April
First Cuckoo Day

In Sussex, England, April 14 is officially known as First Cuckoo Day and heralds the arrival of Spring. It is believed that those who hear the first cuckoo cry will be blessed with good luck and good fortune for the rest of the year. Over the years, there has been a good deal of light-hearted rivalry surrounding the question of where and when the first cuckoo will be heard. Many omens are drawn from the first call heard: lucky if to your right, unlucky if to your left or behind you or if you have not yet eaten. If you have money in your pocket at the time you will have plenty all year (especially if you turn to the right and jingle it), but if not, you will stay poor. If you are in bed, this foreshadows an illness; if you are standing on grass, you will have good fortune.

One popular custom among 19th-century workmen was to stop work upon hearing the first cuckoo, claim the day as a holiday, and go off to drink ale or beer outdoors to welcome the bird.

The cuckoo's habit of laying its eggs in the nests of other birds explains why its cry was regarded, in medieval times, as mocking the cuckold husbands—they would have to bring up another man's child. In some areas, the cuckoo was associated with stupidity and in northern dialects 'gowk' means both *cuckoo* and *fool*.

15 and 16 April
Tellus Mater

The Italian deity Tellus Mater—mother of the earth—was honored on this day. She was a very early fertility deity (later associated with Jupiter) who watched over marriage, the procreation of children, and the fruitfulness of the soil. Her festival was managed by the pontifices and the Vestal Virgins, at which a pregnant cow was sacrificed to ensure plenty throughout the year. In more modern times, this day is traditionally devoted to prayer for the continued health of our environment.

A Simple Prayer of Gratitude

Without Thy sunshine, and Thy rain,
We would not have the golden grain;
Without Thy love we'd not be fed,
We thank thee Lady for our daily bread.

17 April
Rain Festival

Held in Nepal, this annual religious festival of the *Chariot of the Rain God* pays homage to Machendrana, the powerful Indian God of rain. The festival lasts for eight weeks, during which prayers and offerings ensure the God's protection for the region—and especially the temples.

18 and 19 April
Rama's Day

Rama is the seventh Avatar of Vishnu, the Vedic sun God who is reborn each morning and sustains the order of the cosmos. As does Apollo, the Greek sun God, Vishnu rises from the sea where he sleeps during Brahma's night. As an Avatar, Rama descends to earth and assumes a visible form. Rama or Rama-Chandra is a "Moon Rama" or "Gentle Rama" in contrast to some of the more war-oriented Rama. In India, it is believed that the Avatars walk about the earth and work for the good of humanity by defeating the forces of evil and helping the good.

Magickal Activity
Mirror Magick

One of the symbols of Rama is the mirror, the symbol of truth, self-knowledge, and wisdom. As a moon deity, Rama reflects the glory of Vishnu, much in the same way the moon reflects the splendor of the sun. Magickally, the mirror reflects the true identity of the human soul and can be used to divine the future.

The most versatile mirror for magickal work is full length, has three panels, and provides a view of three sides of an image at once. When this triple reflective quality is combined with candlelight, it creates a very mystical effect.

Stand the mirror in the corner of a darkened room and place a lighted candle before each panel. Position a chair facing the center panel. Sit in the chair, take several deep breaths, and relax. Stare fixedly at the reflected image of the center candle flame, pose your question, and look deep into the mirror. The mirror will begin to cloud or fog with a swirling veil of ethereal mist. Through the mist, an image will appear and answer your query. When the image begins to fade, so will the mist. Once the mirror is clear, extinguish the candles, cover the mirror with a dark blue or black velvet drape, and record the experience in your magickal journal or Book of Shadows.

20 April
Shad Planking

During the 1950s in rural America, outdoor political rallies were commonly held preceding elections. They were usually highlighted by flamboyant oratory, hard liquor, and regional food prepared outdoors. Sponsored by local lodges and sports-men's clubs, huge barbecue pits were assembled that could service the entire community. Chicken and rockfish were grilled directly over the fire, but the shad was tacked to planks and placed next to the coals rather than over them. The shad was basted no less than 15 times and cooked to perfection. In some areas of Virginia, this festival is still celebrated, and, although it has been opened to women and Republicans, it still remains the province of the gentlemen and Democrats.

21 April
Parilia

The festival of Parilia, or Pales, was annually held on April 21. Connected with the birth of Rome, this festival was for the purification of sheep and shepherds. The sheep pens were cleaned and decorated with greenery. Large bonfires were built, and the sheep were ritually purified in their smoke, as were the shepherds. The festival came to a close with offerings of milk and sweet cakes for Pales.

22 April
Earth Day

Dedicated to the Earth Mother Gaia, this day marks the time we remember our responsibility toward the environment.

The first Earth Day was celebrated in 1970, as a result of the growing interest in and concern for the ecology movement. Some things that come to mind on this day are recycling, using solar energy, and cleaning up regional parks and waterways to make them safe for Summer activities.

23 April
Vinalia Priora

Vinalia Priora was one of the two major agricultural festivals held in Rome. It was held annually on April 23 and was connected with wine production. *Vinalia* is derived from *vinum* (wine). Originally held in honor of the God Jupiter, this festival later was connected with the Goddess Venus.

The wine casks filled in the previous Aautumn were opened, and the first draft of the new wine was offered as a libation to Jupiter. During this time outside the *Porta Collina* offerings were made to Venus from the female prostitutes of Roma.

Quick Woodruff Wine (for Beltane on 30 April)
1 cup crushed woodruff leaves
½ gallon white wine (Almaden, Mountain Rhine)
1 tsp. sugar
2 cups fresh strawberries

In a small saucepan, bring 1 cup of the wine to a boil. Turn off the heat, and add the sugar and the crushed woodruff leaves. Cover and allow to steep for one hour. Add the mixture to the bottle of white wine. Cover and refrigerate for one week. Pour the wine into a large punch bowl and add the strawberries. You may also serve in individual wine glasses into which a strawberry has been added.

24 April
St. George's Day

St. George is the patron saint of England—as well as Greece, Portugal, and Aragon—and of soldiers and boy scouts. As are most of the saints, George was a mysterious character. He was reputed to have rescued the daughter of the king of Silene—the end of the third century A.D. The princess was a sacrificial victim being offered to a dragon that was devouring the people. Saint George arrived on his white horse and beheaded the dragon with one swift blow of his mighty sword.

During the late medieval period this date was widely celebrated throughout London, Norwich, Chester, Leicester, and York. The festivities began on the evening of the 23rd and proceeded throughout the following day. There were civic presentations, parades, and horse races. It was believed that if you dreamed of a man on this night, he would become your true love.

25 April
The Robigalia

"Warding off" was the entire purpose of this festival, celebrated annually on April 25. It focused on the deity Robigus, whose main attribute was the ability to destroy the dreaded rust or red mildew, a scourge that sometimes attacked the corn (the city's principle food crop). As this deity was associated with the God Mars, all of this day's activities were overseen by the Flamen Martialis, including the offerings of sheep and a red dog to appease Robigus.

26 and 27 April
African Fertility Festival

In many African republics, this New Year's Day celebrates the ancient seed-sowing ceremony performed in honor of the Goddess of fertility, Mawu. Associated with the moon, Mawu is considered to be cool and gentle. She is the creatrix who made people from clay and brings abundance to the land. In some areas, Mawu (moon) is combined with Lisa (sun) to create a dynamic union between the two controlling factors of universe for the protection of crops and people.

28 April–3 May
Floralia

On April 28, 238 B.C., the Romans dedicated their first temple to the Goddess Flora. At the time there had been a food shortage, and, according to the Sibylline Books, the dedication of a temple to the Goddess would ward of the impending famine.

The festival was designed to ensure that the crops blossomed well, so that the harvest would be good. The games and festivities lasted for six days, to May 3. It began with theatrical performances and ended with circus games and a sacrifice to Flora.

The Floralia came to be regarded by prostitutes as their feast. The games drew crowds of commoners, and prostitutes were more licentious than during the Saturnalia—December 17 to 23.

30 April
Beltane/Walpurgis Night

Beltane is celebrated on April 30th (May Eve) and is primarily a fire and fertility festival. Beltane, meaning "Bel-Fire," is derived from the Celtic God Bel, also known as Beli or Balor, which simply means "Lord." Some seem to think that Bel was comparable to the Celtic Gaul God, Cernunnos. This is possible, as most male Gods relate to the sun and fire aspects.

Beltane was the time of the May Queen, when a young woman was chosen from her village to represent the Earth Goddess and reflect the transformation of maiden to mother. In addition, this was the time of the kindling of the Need Fire, when all fires in the village were extinguished and then ritually relit the following day.

Fertility played an important role at Beltane, as it did with all Spring celebrations. The principle symbol of this Sabbat was the May Pole, also known as the *axis mundi*, around which the universe revolved. The pole personified the thrusting masculine force, and the disk at the top depicted the receptive female. There were seven colored ribbons tied to the pole representing the seven colors of the rainbow.

Walpurgis, named after Walburga, an Englishwoman who became the abbess of an eighth-century monastery that housed both men and women. It is believed that before she took up the habit, she was a Germanic moon Goddess, possibly Walpurga—hence her association with May Eve and Witches. (See Appendix A for a Beltane ritual.)

Magickal Activities
Flower Wreath

Items needed: Floral wire and tape; fresh daisies and
carnations; seven different colored ribbons,
6 to 8 inches in length.

Begin by making a circle out of the wire that will sit atop your head. Twist the ends together and cover with a bit of tape. Lay the first flower on the wire and secure with the floral tape. Place the second flower next to the first and secure with the tape. Continue this process until the wire frame is almost completely covered. Leave a ½-inch space between the first and last flowers to tie the ribbons from. Tie each ribbon individually so that it hangs from the back of the crown.

Maypole Center Piece

Items needed: A 12-inch-tall wooden dowel approximately
1½ inches diameter; one 4-inch-diameter disk
and one 2-inch-diameter disk; one small jar
of Petal Porcelain fabric stiffener; seven
different colored 13-inch strips of ribbon;
green paint; wood glue; silk flowers.

The 4-inch disk will serve as the base of your maypole. Pound a small nail through it to affix the dowel to the base. Use a small amount wood glue to secure. Glue the smaller disk to the top. When the glue has dried, paint the entire thing green. Glue the end of each ribbon to the top of the smaller disk, spacing them evenly. Glue the silk flowers to the top of the maypole. Use the Petal Porcelain to stiffen the ribbons so they will stand out and hold their shape.

May

Traditionally May is the "Merry Month," from the old German *murgjaz* or *mirth*. It was named after the Greek *Maia Majestas*, Goddess of Spring, of which the Irish Celtic Queen Medb (Maeve) was an incarnation. The Anglo-Saxon name for May was *Thrimilcmonath*, thrice-milk, due to the abundance of milk that the cows gave at this time.

This fifth month of the Gregorian calendar, and third month of Spring, was when fertility was at its peak, a time of ritual promiscuity in old Pagan Europe. In ancient Rome, it was the custom for girls to be given menstruation parties by their mothers to welcome them into the community of women. In Greece, girls who reached puberty at this time were expected to give their dolls in offering on the altar of Aphrodite.

Despite the return of light and life that May brought, many ancient people considered May to be an unlucky time of the year. Mythologists believe this attitude originated with the Romans, who celebrated *Lemuria* at this time—a festival dedicated to placating the discontented dead.

As the days grow longer, May is the perfect time to nurture and work toward achieving those goals inaugurated during the Winter months.

Magickal Themes for May:
> Nurturing, working, dancing, reaffirming goals

Magickal Correspondences:

Colors:	Green, yellow, white
Food:	Edible flowers, cheese, quiche, oatmeal
Plants:	Woodruff, basil
Stones:	Emerald, jade, lapis-lazuli
Symbols:	Maypole, basket, bonfire
Full Moon:	Hare Moon

1 May
May Day

> *Nature is often hidden; sometimes overcome;*
> *seldom extinguished.*
> —Sir Francis Bacon

Common in Europe and North America, May Day is celebrated by the crowning of the May Queen; dancing around the maypole; and mumming from house to house carrying blossoms and soliciting gifts of food. Most of the activities that take place on May Day symbolize Spring, relating human fertility to crop fertility and rebirth. In the past it was common for young people to pair up, often by lot, and then gather in the woods all May Eve night.

In English folklore, *May Day*, *Bringing in The May*, and *Going-a-Maying* refers to the practice of going out into the countryside to gather flowers and greenery, much of which was used to adorn the May Queen. Bringing in the May remained a staple tradition throughout most of the 16th century, before it was banned by the Protestant reform-fundamentalists who took moral outrage at the unchaperoned activities of the young people. May Day was banned, along with many other traditional customs in the Commonwealth period, but returned after the Restoration.

Today, many of the old customs still prevail, such as woodland weddings and the gathering of morning dew for skin renewal. Horse racing, parades, and dancing around the maypole have made a comeback, as have garland parties and mumming.

2 May
Apple Blossom Festival

The Apple Blossom Festival is one of the oldest flower fairs in the United States. Annually held in Washington State, this welcoming back of Spring heralds from New Zealand and celebrates the blossoming of the apple orchards.

With a rich and colorful history, the apple has been treasured by almost every culture of the world. The ancient Egyptians offered apples to Hapy, the God of the Nile. Norse priests were forbidden to eat apples, due to the fruit's legendary lustful properties. Apples are still offered to the God *Chango,* in the religion of Santeriá, for his continued blessings and protection.

3 and 4 May
Festival of Bona Dea

Bona Dea is the Roman Goddess of the earth and bountiful blessings. In ancient times, her festival was held in secret, usually in the house of the officiating counsel or praetor of the city. Presided over by the mistress of the household, selected matrons, and the Vestal Virgins, special ceremonies were enacted at night for the benefit of the city and its inhabitants.

This festival was for *women only,* to the extent that all statues and paintings of male deities and male members of the household were covered with veils. The room where the ceremonies took place was decorated with vine branches and fresh flowers. Wine was served but called milk, and the covered jar containing it was referred to as *the honey pot.*

Magickal Activity
Wishing Pot

Items needed: A small ceramic jar or pot with a tight-fitting lid; 2" square piece of parchment paper; a gold ink pen; a jar of honey; three silver coins.

Write out your wish on the parchment paper. Place the paper in the bottom of the jar. Add the coins and fill the jar with honey. Cover with the lid. Hold the jar close to your heart and the chant the following nine times to empower the wishing pot:

> *Goddess of blessings and bountiful earth*
> *To my wishes and dreams give birth.*

Place the pot on your altar until your wish comes true. Once you receive your petition, toss the pot into the nearest water way.

5 and 6 May
Cinco de Mayo

For several days, Mexicans and Mexican-Americans commemorate the defeat of the French by *General Ignacio Zaragoza* at the Battle of Pueblo in 1862. His defense of the city dealt a major blow to Napoleon III's attempt to establish a permanent French colony in Central America, which eventually led to the expulsion of the French from Mexico.

In California, Cinco de Mayo is still celebrated and serves to perpetuate Mexican nationalism in a foreign land. All of the pageant's activities, speeches, songs, and events are played out in Spanish, usually beneath the American flag that is flown alongside the Mexican flag.

7 May
Thargelia

Held on the sacred island of *Delos* in ancient Greece, the Thargelia honored Apollo and Artemis. This was a festival of prophecy, music, medicine, and poetry. There were processions, offerings of first fruits, and elaborate musical contests. A youth, with both parents living, was chosen to carry an olive branch, entwined with white and purple wool and hung with figs, acorns, and a vessel of wine to the sanctuary of Apollo. This elaborate offering stayed in the shrine until the next Thargelia, at which time it was replaced by a new branch, adorned with fresh fruits and wine.

8 May
Helston Furry Dance

One of the most famous of all traditional British festivals is Floral or Flora Day or more correctly as the "Furry"—from the Cornish "fer" (Latin *feria*), a fair, rejoicing holyday. The date of the festival coincides with the feast of the Apparition of St. Michael the archangel, Helston's patron saint. The legend recounts that the first furry was danced to celebrate Michael's deliverance from a boulder hurled at him during an altercation with Satan. However, it is quite possible that some of the fair's activities are linked to far older celebrations that honored the Celtic Horned God in the guise of Robin Hood.

From the street dancing that takes place on this day, it is clear that the festival has become inextricably intermingled with May Day. The procession begins at noon with the furry dance. One hundred and fifty couples participate in the dance, which winds through the streets of the town, gardens, and even homes that have left their doors open for the dancers. In the past, it was believed that the dancers would bring good luck and good fortune to the household as they passed through.

9–13 May
Lemuria

In ancient Rome, May 9 through 11 was Lemuria. This was a time of great consequence and set aside to appease the spirits of the household dead, who were believed to be particularly active during the month of May. It seems that the most terrifying of the wandering apparitions were those of children who had died young, because they apparently harbored ill feelings for the living. The head of the household would rise at midnight and make the mana fico sign (the thumb between the middle of the closed fingers). He would then walk barefoot through the house and scatter black beans as a ransom so ghosts or spirits would leave the other household members alone. Otherwise, they might be carried off.

Little is known of the public rites that took place at this time, except that all state affairs were in abeyance, no battles were fought, no business was conducted, and no marriages were contracted. It is, however, believed that the sacrifices made to Mania (mother of the Lares) on May 11 might have been part of the Lemuria, because Mania was a Goddess of death.

Magickal Activity
Protection Bag

Items needed: A small black bag; one each of the following stones: cat's eye, flint, jet, obsidian, olivine, and onyx; 10 black beans; one black votive candle (in a holder).

Light the votive candle. Chant the following as you place the stones in the bag one at a time:

> *To any who shall cause me harm,*
> *Your powers I now disarm.*

Place the bag full of stones next the candle. Allow the candle to burn out. Carry the bag in your purse or brief case, or place it near the main entrance of your home.

14 May
Rain Ceremony/
Festival of the Midnight Sun

The rain ceremonies in Guatemala take place around this time every year. The exact date is determined through divination by local priests and tribal leaders. Once the five-day festival begins, the Gods (both Pagan and Christian) are invoked for aid. Prayers are offered at village churches and at the numerous mountaintop shrines that dot the countryside, in the hopes of persuading the Gods to grant rain for a bountiful harvest.

In northern Scandinavia, May 14 begins a 10-week celebration that pays homage to the Goddess of the sun, *Dag,* whose name means "Day" (one who shines so brightly that she illuminates both the heavens and the earth). Thus begins the 10 consecutive weeks of daylight experienced in the extreme North.

15 May
Festival of Maia, Vesta, and Mercury

Today was sacred to the ancient Roman Goddess Maia, Goddess of Spring, and the wife of Vulcan. She was connected with fertility and the growth of all living things. Over time, she became confused with the Greek Goddess of the same name, who was the mother of Hermes, and the equivalent of the Roman Mercury.

On this day in ancient Rome, the Vestal Virgins (priestesses of Vesta) performed special ceremonies to regulate the water supply for the coming Summer. The rites were considered critical to the survival of Rome and the propagation of its crops. Additionally, this was the day when Roman citizens paid tribute to Mercury, the God of commerce and the marketplace. This was a prominent day of celebration, because Mercury's help was considered crucial to maintaining the growing foreign trade that the Empire enjoyed and depended on.

16 May
St. Brendan the Navigator

The voyages of St. Brendan the Navigator are legendary. An Irish Celtic priest, he is believed to be the first European to set foot on American soil. It was during the sixth century that he set sail in search of the Garden of Eden. His voyage lasted seven years and 40 days and produced an extensive itinerary of rich adventure.

It is believed that St. Brendan found the garden island he sought, only to be forbidden to come ashore. Countless medieval maps were based upon his stories, and some say that other adventurous souls tried to retrace his steps only to fail and be lost at sea. It is even hypothesized that that St. Brendan might have been the inspiration behind the voyages of Christopher Columbus—who had long admired his work.

17 May
Seminole Green Corn Dance

The Green Corn Dance is the principle ceremony of the Florida Seminoles and provides them with a recreational diversion to celebrate the planting, ripening, and harvesting of the corn. Although many of the customs of the Seminoles are of recent origin, the Green Corn Dance is a very old festival that is celebrated by the Cherokee, Natchez, and Creek Indians as well. One of the highlights of the festival is the *Feather Dance*, which is performed in the morning and immediately following lunch. Each participant of the dance holds a white egret feather attached to a long pole that is then held tight against the left shoulder. The dance is performed by the men only and pays homage to the four quarters of the ceremonial grounds where the festivities are being held. In addition to sacred dances, there are ball games, council meetings, the naming of youths that have come of age, and a feast of barbequed beef. The festival concludes with the drinking of a black beverage made from a creek holly shrub, which is believed to purge the body of all sin.

18 May
Apollo's Day

This day is sacred to the Greco-Roman God Apollo, who embodied the qualities most admired by ancient Greek society. Associated with human intellect, musical harmony, religious purity, and male beauty, he was considered to be "the most Greek of the Gods."

Apollo personified the Greek male. Annually on his day, 17-year-old males were initiated and welcomed into the community.

The giving of advice was related to Apollo through the *giving of prophecy*. Inscribed on the wall at Delphi (the most famous of all Greek oracles) are two of his most memorable proverbs: "Nothing In Excess" and "Know Thyself." In addition to Delphi, Apollo's second-most important sanctuary was the tiny Aegean island of *Delos*, believed to be the place of his birth. As a primary God of the Greeks, Apollo oversaw human religious purification and spiritual atonement. He was considered to be a patron of medicine and the lord of music.

Magickal Activity
Sun Talisman for Personal Power

Items needed: Yellow paper or card stock; a gold marker or ink pen; first pentacle of the sun (pictured).

This simple rite is best performed at high noon on Sunday. Inscribe the first pentacle of the sun on the yellow paper using the gold marker. Cut the pentacle out and hold it toward the sun. Feel the power and energy of the sun flow through you and into the pentacleas you chant:

> *Glory of the sun, everlasting light,*
> *Bring me power, strength and might.*
> *So mote it be!*

Carry the pentacle in your purse or wallet.

19 and 20 May
The Hammer of Thor

For those who follow the Nordic traditions, May 19 and 20 are dedicated to the Hammer of Thor, *Mjöllnir* (the crusher).

The Hammer of Thor is a symbolic tool that discharges the power of *right orderliness* over that of the power of *harmful chaos*.  According to mythology, one activity that was undertaken at this time was the ritual of trial by combat, where the will of the Gods would decide which combatant had goodness on his side. Today, devotees of Thor wear small hammer pendants as symbols of their dedication to the Scandinavian sky God of thunder and patron of sailors, farmers, and the poorer classes.

21 May
The Agnoalia / Festival of Vediovis

The ancient Roman *Agnoalia* was held on January 9 and May 21 possibly for Janus. It seems that even the Romans were a bit confused about the particular feast day. However, just to be on the safe side, on each occasion, a ram was sacrificed at the Regia. Other than that, little is known about the *Agnoalia.*

Vediovis or *Vedius* was a Roman God closely connected with the God Jupiter. However, he was considered to be the opposite of Jupiter and therefore associated with things that were harmful, including the Underworld. Originally, Vedius was a deity of the swamps and volcanic activity. There were several temples to Vedius, and annually on this date a she-goat was sacrificed to him to placate the eruptive forces of Nature and the Underworld.

22 May
Ragnar Lodbrok

Remembered on this day, Ragnar Lodbrok was a leader of the Vikings who was captured by the Christian Northumbrians, tortured, and thrown into a pit of poisonous snakes. It was Ragnar's death song, of his faith in the afterlife, that inspired a bard present at the execution to convey his message to others. Passed from generation to generation, the song provides reassurance and hope for what lies in the great beyond:

> *The Disir call me back home, those whom Odin has sent for me from the Hall of the Lord of Hosts. Gladly will I sup ale in the high seat with the Gods. The days of my life are finished. I laugh as I die!*

23 May
The Rosalia

The Rosalia is another of the ancient Roman festivals that are so plentiful in the merry month of May. This one was sacred to the Springtime flower Goddess Flora and to Venus, the Goddess of love. Flowers were plentiful at this time, especially roses, which were used for all manner of perfumes, cosmetics, and tea.

Rose Body Splash

3 cups spring or distilled water   2 cups fresh rose petals
½ tsp. essential rose oil

Heat water to a boil. Add flower petals and simmer for
15 minutes. Turn heat off and allow to steep for one hour.
Strain off plant material and pour into a glass bottle with a
tight-fitting cap and refrigerate until ready to use.

24 May
The Mothers or Three Marys

This French holy day celebrates the cult of the Goddess
as a triad of mothers at Aries, in Provence. Also referred to as
"The Three Marys of Provence" or "Three Marys of the Sea,"
this ancient festival acknowledges the three phases of woman-
hood as a triad, from birth, through life, to death. It was common for husbands to give flowers and candy to their daughters,
wives, and mothers at this time.

25 May
Festival of Fortuna

Fortuna was probably originally a fertility Goddess, and rites to her would have reflected this concept. However, as she became associated with the Greek Tyche, her persona changed to that of a Goddess of fate, chance, and luck.

Fortuna's main symbol is the wheel upon which she stands, implying the instability of human fortune. Her most recog-nized symbols are those of the cornucopia and rudder, indicating her ability to steer the destiny of people. At this time of year, her temples would have been decorated with fresh flowers. Offerings would have been made to her for the purpose of bringing good fortune and luck to those who followed her ways.

26–28 May
Sacred Well Day/Well Dressing

May 26 is well-dressing day in dozens of European villages. Celebrations may vary from town to town, but the actual dressing of wells remains consistent with tradition.

A large shallow wooden tray, up to 12 feet long, is packed with smooth soft clay. Elaborate pictures or patterns are made by pressing thousands of flower petals into the clay, plus other natural items, including moss, stones, and shells. The trays are then mounted on scaffolding behind, around, or across the well. In addition to the panel, the wells are decorated with ribbons and fresh flower garlands. It is believed that the spirits of the well enjoy this practice and that, if placated, they will continue to bless the water with healing properties.

29 May
Oak Apple Day

This popular British festival is held annually on May 29 and commemorates the return of King Charles II from exile. It was on this day in 1660 that Charles made his triumphant return to London, thus ending the English Republic and Cromwell's puritanical horrors. Celebrations include the ringing of bells, church services, bonfires, and the tossing of eggs at anyone not wearing an oak leaf.

From the very beginning, the essential elements of this festival have rested with the boughs of oak leaves—a representation of the oak in which Charles had hidden from Parliamentary troops after his defeat at Worcester (in 1651). However, it is also possible that much of the tradition that is still held comes from a far older time, when worship of the oak was perpetuated by various Pagan cults.

30 May
Memorial Day

The origins of Memorial Day, or Decoration Day, as it was first known, are remote and mixed. In rural America, the custom of cleaning the cemeteries and decorating graves was an occasion for reunions and picnics. It is possible that this legal holiday grew from the more ancient and widespread festivals of the dead, such as that of the Japanese *Obon* or *Festival of Lanterns* when the graves of ancestors are ritually cleaned and decorated. Historically, it seems that Memorial Day grew up almost spontaneously from a need to pay homage to the dead, especially those who gave of their lives in a patriotic fashion.

General order No. 11 from General John A. Logan, dated May 5, 1868, begins: *The 30th of May 1868 is designated for the purpose of strewing with flowers, or otherwise decorating the graves of comrades who died in defense of their country during the late rebellion.... In 1966 by Congressional resolution and presidential proclamation Waterloo, New York, was designated the "birthplace" of Memorial Day.*

June

June is named after *Juno* (the Greek *Hera)*, the multi-faceted Roman moon—Mother Goddess who was honored at the *Vestalia.* At this time of the year, processions of women would make a pilgrimage to the temple to ask the Goddess to bless their households. In ancient Greece, this was the month of the *Skirophorion,* when the Mother Goddess Athene was worshiped at the Parthenon. In ancient Mesopotamia, the cult of Inanna/Ishtar climaxed with a Midsummer festival of epic proportions.

The month of June is "the door of the year" and ushers in the Summer—the season of growth and abundance and a time of maximum light and minimum darkness. Governed by the astrological signs Gemini and Cancer, June is considered the best month for beginning partnerships and marriage.

This is the month set aside to strengthen and consolidate gains. June opens to let the sunshine in on new opportunities. Symbolically, this is the time of year to put the maximum amount of effort into those goals you want to manifest by first harvest.

Magickal Themes for June:
Growth, cultivating, rejoicing

Magickal Correspondences:

Colors:	Bright yellow, gold, dark green
Food:	Berries, oranges, beans, pork
Plants:	Sunflower, mugwort, marigold
Stones:	Agate, adventurine
Symbols:	Wheel, chariot, floating candles
Full Moon:	Dyad Moon

1 June

All life, even in its lowest form, is energy.
—Plontinus

Traditionally, the first day of June was set aside for the festival of *Carna*, the Roman Goddess of door hinges, and thus domestic life. She was thought to dwell in a sacred wood called *Lucus Helerni*, on the banks of the Tiber River. It was there that sacrifices were made to Carna by the pontiffs to ensure the well-being of the community.

Carna also held responsibility for the protection of the people from vampires that took the form of semi-human birds who tried to suck the blood of unattended newborn babies. According to Robert Graves *The White Goddess,* it was only the priestess who cooked her feast food of white beans and pork, that served during the festivities.

White Bean and Wilted Greens Soup

1 can cooked cannellini beans,
　drained and rinsed
2 cups vegetable stock
　(Swanson's Vegetable Broth)

1 clove garlic,
　peeled and chopped
1 cup chopped Swiss chard
½ teaspoon salt

In a 2-quart sauce pan, bring the beans, garlic, and stock to a boil. Reduce heat and simmer 10 to 15 minutes. With a slotted spoon, scoop out the beans and transfer to a blender with ½ cup of the liquid. Purée until smooth. Return the purée to the saucepan and stir until blended. Add the chopped greens, season with salt, and cook for another 5 minutes. Serves 2.

2 June
Mother Shipton's Day/St. Elmo's Day

Dedicated to Mother Shipton, this day still provokes centuries old controversy: Was Mother Shipton a gifted prophet or a child of the devil and, therefore, a Witch? According to the legend, Mother Shipton (Ursula Sontheil) was born in Knaresborough (Yorkshire) in 1488 and foretold many of the major events in English history. She eventually became the patron saint of working women, especially those of the lower classes employed in laundries and kitchens.

St. Elmo was a Syrian bishop and the patron saint of sailors. The electrical discharges—St. Elmo's Fire—that flicker around ships during storms at this time of the year are believed to be a sign of his protection.

3 June
Festival of Bellona

In ancient Rome, this day was set aside to worship the Bellona, the Goddess of war and personification of force. Equated with *Enyo*, the Greek Goddess of combat, Bellona was sometimes regarded as the wife or sister of Mars. She was portrayed as driving her own chariot, with a sword and a spear or torch in each of her hands. Her temple in Rome was dedicated in 296 B.C. by *Appius Claudius Caccus* during a battle against the Etrucans and Sammites. Because the temple was situated just outside the wall of Rome, it was often used by the Senate for meetings and to receive foreign ambassadors.

Directly in front of the temple stood the *columna bellica* (column of war). Before a war could be declared on a foreign enemy, a priest would hurl a spear over the column in the direction of the enemy territory. This practice continued up until the time of Marcus Aurelius.

Magickal Activity
Protection Charm

For this you will need the fourth pentacle of Mars (pictured), laminated with plastic, and a bowl of salt water. Slowly sprinkle some salt water over the seal as you chant the following charm:

> *Elements of earth and sea,*
> > *Return to all by power of three.*
> *That which may be sent to me,*
> > *Unless I have summoned it to be.*
> *I am protected from this night,*
> > *By the spirits of power and might.*

Wear the pentacle for protection on a daily basis. Once a month, at the dark of the moon, repeat the charm to keep your pentacle properly charged.

4 June
Whitsuntide/Whitsun/White Sunday

White Sunday, or Whitsun, is the English name for the *Feast of Pentecost*, when the Holy Spirit was believed to descend in tongues of flame on the Apostles, thus endowing them with the knowledge of languages they needed to do their work. The name White Sunday was given to this day because of the white robes that were worn by the priests who took their vows on this day.

A moveable feast, this is one of the grandest in the Christian calendar. Churches, homes, and spiritual sites are decorated with flowers, and friends and family gather for cheerful outdoor activities. In Scotland, fund-raising events, games, and Morris dancers add to the festivities. Some customs include tug-of-war, bread-throwing, and cheese-rolling, followed by a feast of roast veal, pigeon pie, gooseberry tart, and Yorkshire cheesecake.

5 June
World Environment Day

Established in 1972, World Environment Day was created to increase our awareness of the planet. Themes include: what can be done to reduce pollution; how people can help ensure that Mother Nature's greatest creatures are protected from extinction; and what can be done to restore natural resources. This is a great day to gather friends and family together to clean up a local park or roadside, followed by a "job well done" cookout and picnic.

6 June
The Egungun Festival

In Nigeria, this is the first day of a weeklong celebration held in honor of the ancestors. *Egungun* or *Egun* is the Yoruba word used to describe those ancestors or souls that have moved on—traveled beyond the physical realm. It is believed that the *eguns* exist on another level or plane of consciousness for the purpose of overseeing human activities.

Similar to ancient Egyptian burial customs, the Nigerians conduct what are considered to be *honorable rites*—special ceremonies that provide the dead with the tools they will need to conduct meaningful work in the spirit world. They will also receive offerings of food, cooked according to tradition that contain the items they most favored.

During the weeklong celebration, the people participate in elaborate processions and undulating dances and sing devout songs to those who have passed on. It is also a custom to dress up in costumes, and reenact the stories or legends connected with the more prominent ancestors. In exchange for the veneration paid to them, the ancestors offer protection, wisdom through divination, and prosperity for those who honor them.

Magickal Activity
The Ancestor Altar

It is believe that coffee keeps the ancestors alert. Candles attract them, water refreshes them, and flowers please them.

Items needed: A small table covered with a white cloth; seven glasses of water; one white 7-day glass candle; framed photographs of deceased relatives; fresh flowers; a cup filled with strong black coffee.

Place the photographs at the back of the altar with the glasses of water in front of them. The flowers and candle are placed in the center of the altar, and the coffee center front. To activate your altar, light the candle and say the prayer:

> *O Gentle one who knows all things,*
> *Of boundless love and grace unknown.*
> *Enfold me in thy protective-spreading wings,*
> *And let thy infinite wisdom be known.*

Take a few moments to think about those loved ones whose photographs grace your altar. If you are in need of advice, ask your ancestors for help at this time. Some people keep their Tarot cards on their ancestor altar to provide a vehicle for their loved ones to speak through. When you are finished, allow the candle to burn out. It is considered advantageous to offer a new candle, fresh flowers, water, and coffee on a regular basis.

7–9 June
Vestalia, Festival of Vesta

Vestalia is the spirit of ancient Rome, abided in a flame that was kept flickering in the temple of Vesta—the hearth (heart) of the city and the royal palace. The fire was tended by six priestesses, considered to be the "king's daughters," who were chosen as children for their nobility and physical perfection. The priestesses or *Vestial Virgins* were held in high regard and lived a life of affluence. However, their high position demanded discipline and compromise; they were required to remain celibate for their 30 years of service.

The festival of Vesta began on June 7. When the temple was opened to women, men were forbidden to enter the temple. Because very little is known of the public or private Vestal rites, we can only speculate as to what took place. However, historians do know that at some point, the fire in the temple was ritually rekindled and that prayers and offerings were made.

In addition to performing all of the sacred rites for the festival, the Vestals undertook other ritual duties. For example, it was their responsibility to make the sacred salt cake (mola-salsa) used in the Vestalia. This required them to fetch water from a sacred spring and bring it back without setting it down along the way. They were also in charge of ritually sweeping the temple clean before it was closed to outsiders on June 15.

Magickal Activity
Invocation for Vesta

Items needed: A small table covered with a white cloth; a statue or picture of Vesta; one large white pillar candle; fresh violets; a dish of salt; a dish of flour.

Place the statue or picture of Vesta near the center-back of the altar. The candle should go directly in front of the statue, and the violets are sprinkled around the candle. The two small dishes of salt and flour are placed center-front.

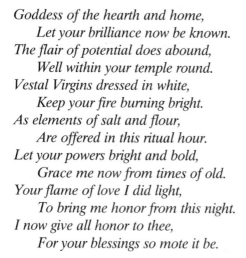

To begin, take several relaxing breaths and focus on the image of Vesta. Imagine how it might have been to be one of her priestesses. When you feel the time is right, light the candle and speak her invocation:

> *Goddess of the hearth and home,*
> > *Let your brilliance now be known.*
> *The flair of potential does abound,*
> > *Well within your temple round.*
> *Vestal Virgins dressed in white,*
> > *Keep your fire burning bright.*
> *As elements of salt and flour,*
> > *Are offered in this ritual hour.*
> *Let your powers bright and bold,*
> > *Grace me now from times of old.*
> *Your flame of love I did light,*
> > *To bring me honor from this night.*
> *I now give all honor to thee,*
> > *For your blessings so mote it be.*

When you have completed the invocation, take some time to reflect on the Goddess. If you have prayers or petitions of your own, make them at this time. Leave the candle to burn for one hour. Daily lighting of the candle will bring Vesta's blessings to your home and family.

10 June
The Beginning of Duir (Oak Month)

According to Celtic tradition, this is the beginning of Duir, the month of the oak. The oak is the most sacred tree of the Druids and a symbol of life at its peak. This is a time of empowerment, as Duir signifies the door of the year that opens to admit all good things. This is a good time to hug a tree in appreciation for the abundance of light and life Mother Earth has provided.

11 June
Matralia and Festival of Fortuna

In ancient Rome, the Goddess *Matuta* was connected to fertility and Nature. Her festival, the Matralia, was held on June 11 and was presided over entirely by women. It is interesting to note that only free women were allowed to enter her temple and participate in her rituals. There was one exception: A free woman could bring a slave girl into the outer sanctuary of the temple, but only if she slapped the slave's face before entering.

Matuta's temple was in the *Forum Boarium*, alongside one for Fortuna, who was also worshiped on this day. Fortuna was an especially popular deity, and her festivals were celebrated with great enthusiasm. Rome was filled with statues of Fortuna, and monuments were constantly being erected in her honor. Although little is known about what actually took place at some of these ancient festivals, we do know that they were times for the people to renew their relationship with the Gods. There would have been elaborate rites, a sacrifice, and games presided over by state officials. And it was held by all that the failure to celebrate a festival would cause the Gods to cease being benevolent.

12 June
Rice Festival

Still a popular event, the Korean Rice Festival ensures an abundant rice harvest. The custom of washing one's hair in a stream on this day is believed to dispel bad luck and ward off evil. The traditional meal for this festival is one of fresh fish, steamed rice, and greens.

13 June
Feast of Epona

This was an ancient Celtic festival that celebrated the sacredness of the horse and the Goddess Epona—the spirit of movement, fertility, and war. So popular was Epona that she was the only known Celtic Goddess to have been honored in Rome, where she was often called Epona Augusta or Regina and invoked on behalf of the Emperor. Images and bas-reliefs of Epona show her riding a horse sidesaddle and occasionally lying half-naked along the back of one. She is usually carrying a cornucopia and goblet, representations of her fertility aspect.

In all probability, her festival would have been a "Horse Fair" and attracted hundreds of participants. There would have been horse races, games, and horse auctions. Most assuredly there would have been no shortage of stout ale and hearty edibles. These types of festivals flourished all over Britain before the Victorian era, at which time they became business auctions and less times of spiritual celebration. Even today, from June 13 through September 30, horse fairs dot the English countryside, providing people with a time of celebration and relaxation.

The Horse

Attributes: Swift Action, Power
Direction: North, East, South, West
Element: earth, air, fire, water

The horse has long been a symbol of swiftness and power. In ancient mythology it is the horse who bears the heros and the Gods across the earth—and even across the sky at great speed. The horse is physical power and unearthly power. In Shamanic practices, the horse enables the Shaman to fly through the air to reach the heavens or spirit realm. The horse is able to carry great burdens for long distances with ease.

When you need to respond swiftly to a situation, call on the horse. If you need more personal power or are overburdened by too much work, ask the horse to give you more strength and power.

14 June
Vidar's Day

In modern *Asatru*, this day is sacred to Vidar, son of Odin who survives the destruction of Ragnarok. Patron of leatherworkers, Vidar has a stout boot that he puts in the mouth of the demonic Fenris-wolf to kill it. On this day, it was customary for Nordic leatherworkers to put aside all their scraps and then bury them in a pit for Vidar to ward of evil and bad luck.

15 June
St. Vitus's Day

Vitus is the patron saint of Bohemia, and one of the Fourteen Auxiliary Saints. Early legends have him as a child martyr from Lucania or Sicily. However, the later myths retell of his life as an adult. The most popular story has him being boiled in oil, thrown to lions, and stretched on the rack, only to emerge unscathed and die peacefully at home in Lucania. He was said to have caused or cured the *Tanzwut,* or dancing mania, in which wild leaps and gyrations, often to music, led to mass fainting, especially among girls and young women. This spectacle has often been compared to the hysteria that takes place at modern rock concerts. His legacy remains as "St. Vitus's dance," the name given to the nervous disorder or disease technically known as *Sydenham's chorea*. Vitus is the patron saint of dancers, and his emblem is the fighting cock.

16 June
Sun Festival

In some of the more remote areas of Mexico, fragments of this ancient Peruvian festival can be found. To the ancients, the sun represented the supreme cosmic power and an all-seeing deity. When it was coupled with the rain, it gave life to the earth. The Sun Festival was a celebration of power and beauty when the Sky Father and Earth Mother were conjoined in sacred marriage. Great bonfires, ecstatic dancing, and offerings were made to the Gods. Today, these festivals are less elaborate and usually end up being family picnics. However, one custom still remains: to burn one's old clothing to banish sickness and bad luck.

17 and 18 June
Lily Festival

The ancient Shinto festival of the *Cleansing Lily* originated from the need to dispel early summer downpours that would invariably lead to flooding. The lily stalks were gathered at dawn by seven maidens wearing white robes. The stalks were taken to local shrines for blessing. The flowers stayed in these temples overnight, during which time they were prayed over by the priests. Early the next morning, a procession led by the maidens walked through the town's streets, waving the lilies to attract moisture-free weather.

19 June
Juneteenth

This is one of the "freedom days" celebrated in the United States for the end of slavery. It was on June 19, 1863, that General Gordon Granger arrived in Texas—with the avowed intention of enforcing President Lincoln's *Emancipation Proclamation*. June 19, 1865, became freedom day for slaves in east Texas, as General Gordon Granger was finally able to implement the Proclamation and force the slave owners to release their captors. The 19th of June, shortened to *Juneteenth*, became a holiday, and its celebrations spilled over into other states including Alabama and Florida, which were heavily populated with African Americans. The high point of the day was the election of a king and queen to oversee the festivities. The queen was bestowed with the title "Goddess of Liberty."

20, 21, and 22 June
Midsummer Eve/Summer Solstice

The Summer Solstice is celebrated between June 20 and June 22—the longest day and shortest night of the year. The festival of Midsummer venerates the potential of the life-sustaining powers of fire and water, forces that were vital to our ancestors' survival. It was believed that fire would help keep the sun alive and that the blessing of waterwells would continue their flow to nurture the parched earth. Without sun and water, there would be no crops and all would perish.

One of the most popular customs that grew out of the early fertility rites was that of jumping or leaping over Midsummer bonfires. The idea being, the higher one jumped, the higher the crops would grow.

Another symbol that was popularized at this time was the wheel. The turning of the wheel represented the turning or progression of the seasons. Wheels were decorated with brightly colored ribbons and fresh flowers. Lighted candles were placed on them, and then they were set afloat on the lakes and rivers.

Midsummer Eve and Midsummer Night are genuinely thought to be particularly uncanny times. It was reasoned that certain plants were endowed with magickal properties on this night, that, if gathered before sunrise, could be used for protection against all evil spirits and forces.

With the sun at its zenith, Midsummer was, and still is, a time for marriages, family celebrations, and coming-of-age parties.

Symbolically, Midsummer is the time to nurture those goals you made at the beginning of the year as you reflect on the progress you have made toward bringing them into fruition. (See Appendix A for a Midsummer Ritual.)

Magickal Activities
Floating Candles

Midsummer is a celebration of light and life, symbolized by the flame of a candle and the movement of water. A large glass bowl filled with an assortment of floating candles makes a wonderful point of focus for ritual. Choose bright yellow sunflowers, white lilies, and red tulip-shaped candles. Have each person participating in the ritual inscribe his or her desire, with a pin, on a candle. Have each person come forward, place his or her candle in the bowl and light it as he makes his wish. Following the ritual, the bowl is placed outdoors and the candles are left to burn out.

The Sun Wheel

One of the most popular symbols of Midsummer is the Sun Wheel, the turning of which suggests the turning, or progression, of the seasons. The Wheel is decorated with flowers, fresh herbs, and brightly colored ribbons.

The simplest method for making a Sun Wheel is to buy an already-prepared natural-branch wreath from an arts and crafts store. Affix small branches of rowan to form the spokes of the

wheel (four spokes to represent the elements and cross-quarter days or eight to symbolize the eight Wiccan Sabbats). Use floral wire to attach fresh flowers and herbs to the wreath. Embellish with brightly colored ribbons. The wheel can be used as the focal point for your Midsummer rites or hung on the front door of your home for decoration.

23 and 24 June
St. John's Eve and St. John's Day

The feast of St. John the Baptist is unusual because it celebrates his death rather than his birth. St. John has been called the saint of the Summer Solstice, in that his feast has long been associated with that of Midsummer. The superstitious still believe St. John's Eve to be one of the most uncanny and dangerous nights of the year, when all manner of fairies, ghosts, and evil spirits are aboard.

St. John's Day has long been considered the best time to discover one's true love. Generally, the magickal practices that take place on this day are in the form of divination. For example, if you pare an apple round and round without a break in the peeling and then throw the peel over your left shoulder, it will form the initial of your future husband or wife. Place a glass of water directly under the sun's rays, and leave it for one hour. During this time you must sit silently next to the glass. When the time is up, add the white of an egg to the water in the glass. It will spell out the name or occupation of the spouse-to-be.

25 June
Midsummer Bride's Day

In Sweden, June 25 is May Day and when the people of the province *Blekinge* choose their Midsummer Bride or May Queen. A bride is chosen from the town's young women, who will then select a bridegroom. Money is collected for the couple, who are, for the time, looked upon as husband and wife. After the day-long festivities, the money that has been collected is given to the local church and charities.

26 June
Alaskan Whale Dance

In the remote fishing villages of Alaska, fishermen don whale masks and dance from door to door, sharing their whale meat with all who respond. The dance is a celebration to appease the spirits of the whales that have died to provide food for the village. It also helps to ensure an abundant source of food for the coming year.

27 June
Festival of Intium Aestatis/
Death of Julian the Blessed

In ancient Rome, the festival of Intium Aestatis kicked of the beginning of summer in honor of Aestas, the Goddess of Summer.

It was on this day in 363 C.E. that Julian "The Apostate" died from a fatal wound received in battle. Julian was named "The Apostate" by Christian writers because he reinstated the Pagan cults after Christianity had become the established religion of the Roman Empire.

Julian was brought up in Cappadocia and given a Christian education, but he had a passion for the classics and the old Gods. When Julian became emperor, he openly professed his Pagan beliefs and attempted to revive some of the older ideals and a tolerance for *all* religions. Unfortunately, his philosophy did not sit well with the Christian bishops, who were politically influential at the time.

There was little support for Julian's return to Paganism, despite his stand. Furthermore, many of the Roman officials disliked Julian's efforts to improve the lot of the Jews in the Empire or his preparations for a long war with Persia. Julian set out with some 65,000 infantry and cavalry in March 363. He crossed the Syrian desert, capturing small cities along the way. He reached Ctesiphon in June, but it could not be breached. He ordered a tactical retreat up the Tigris. On June 26, he was wounded in a skirmish, and he died on June 27. It is very possible that his death was ordered ahead of time by disgruntled politicians and carried out by one of his own soldiers.

28 and 29 June
St. Peter's Eve and Rushbearing

St. Peter's day, has been a day of *foundations* since the Middle Ages, when the rushes that covered the stone floors of homes and churches were replaced. The actual strewing days developed into ceremonial occasions, centering on the rushbearing procession to the local church.

In northern England, Lancashire, Cheshire, and adjacent Yorkshire, rushbearings were the high points of the year, reaching a pinnacle of splendor in the early 19th century. The focal point of the festivities was on the *rushcart*, with its towering load of green rushes skillfully piled in a pyramid shape. It was secured with flower-woven rush rope, topped by oak boughs, and often hung with glittering silverware and other adornments that showed off the wealth of the community and reflected away ill luck. The great festivals and ceremonies that surrounded rushbearing went into a sharp decline in the late Victorian period. Even in the most remote villages, rushbearing is but a memory of times gone by.

30 June
Dedication Day of the Temple of Hercules

In ancient Rome this was the Dedication day of the temple of Hercules and the Muses. The temple was built by *Marcus*

Fulvius Nobilior out of the fines he had collected as a censor in 179 B.C. It seems that when he was in Greece, he had heard of Hercules, leader of the Muses (normally a function of Apollo). The temple was quite elaborate, and Fulvius set up a calendar inscription, statues of the nine Muses, and one of Hercules playing a lyre. The rites would have included a procession to the temple, prayers, and invocations, climaxing with a sacrifice and games.

July

Until 44 B.C. this month was called *Quintilis;* it was renamed in honor of the murdered Julius Caesar, who had been born on the 12th. In 46 B.C.E. the previous Roman calendar was reorganized with the help of Alexandrian sages to form the new Julian calendar. After a year of chaos and confusion created by the change, the Julian calendar remained the main calendar in the West for the next 1,600 years, when it was replaced by the Gregorian calendar.

This middle-of-the-Summer month is a time of sudden storms and hay-making and is associated with the hot and sultry "dog-days," when the *Sirius-Canciula* (the Dog-Star) rises with the sun, often associated with the Goddess Demeter.

July is a fun-filled month with church fêtes, family gatherings, smoky barbecues, and celebrations that include St. Mary Magdalen, patroness of prostitutes; Saint Anne, mother of the Virgin Mary and the patroness of housewives; and St. Wilgefortis, who supposedly sprouted an immense beard overnight to rid herself of suitors chosen by her father. Magickally, July is a time of personal growth, learning new ways to be creative, and cultivating friendships.

Magickal Themes for July:
Expansion, improvement, meditation

Magickal Correspondences:

Colors:	Silver, amber, saffron-red
Food:	Fruit, vegetables, fish, pork
Plants:	Garlic, nettles, red-poppy, hibiscus
Stones:	Beryl, sapphire, moonstone
Symbols:	Mirror, sickle, spear
Full Moon:	Mead Moon

1 and 2 July

Happiness is not a reward—it is a consequence.
Suffering is not a punishment—it is a result.
— Ralph Ingersoll

For the agricultural communities, this is the beginning of hay season. Spells for continued fair weather are needed to dry out the hay and maturing growing corn.

If the first of July it be rainy weather,
'Twil rain, more or less, for four weeks together.
— Charles Kightly,
Perpetual Almanack of Folklore

In Nepal, this is the festival of *Naga Panchami*, devoted to the Snake-Gods called Nagas. Early on, people lined the streets for the elaborate parades featuring live serpents and flamboyantly costumed participants. Sacred snake images are adorned with flower garlands and displayed on religious altars. As the sun sets, offerings are made at snake holes for the continued fertility of the people and the land.

The serpent has long been a phallic symbol of the procreative male force. Living beneath the earth, it possesses knowledge of the Underworld and the mystical powers of transformation. In many cultures, it is a symbol of death and destruction as well as resurrection. The serpent also represents the  Kundalini force, the potential of light and darkness, and serves as a guardian of thresholds and temples—the protector of esoteric knowledge.

3 July
Festival of Cerridwen

In the rural villages of Wales, the festival of Cerridwen celebrates the fertility of the land and is a reward for the labors of Summer. As a Goddess of grain, the moon, and abundance, Cerridwen represents ingenuity and fortuity. Her major contribution to Celtic mythology rests with her cauldron, around which numerous legends were developed. The cauldron, called Amen, contained a sacred beverage that bestowed creativity and knowledge on all who partook of its contents. Symbolic of the womb, the cauldron still holds a special place within the Wiccan religion as it represents the Mysteries—the inner teachings of creation, transformation, and regeneration.

Magickal Activity
Cauldron Magick

This spell is designed to make a wish come true by reinforcing the desire on a daily basis. Affix a white taper candle to the bottom of a cauldron. Light the candle as you say:

> *Within this cauldron burns the fire,*
> *That will now manifest my desire.*

Concentrate on the flame of the candle, and visualize what it is you desire. Allow the candle to burn for one hour, and then extinguish it. Each day, *at the same time*, light the candle and repeat the chant as you focus on your desire. Allow the candle to burn for one hour. Repeat until your wish comes true.

❖❖❖

4 July
Independence Day

It was after the famous midnight ride of Paul Revere in April 1775 that England's colonies in the New World began their armed conflict against the British Imperial power. By July 2, 1776, the colonies voted for independence from Britain. A document was drawn up stating this intent. On July 4, 1776,  what we know as the *Declaration of Independence* was signed by John Hancock—president of the Continental Congress at Philadelphia—and delegates from the 13 colonies. By the 1880s Independence Day had become a major American holiday.

5 July
Tynwald Ceremony

On July 5 on Tynwald Hill, St. John's, Isle of Man, the people gather to celebrate an old Norse assembly system established more than 1,000 years ago. The ceremony still takes place on the old Norse field of assembly at St. John's, near the center of the island, where there stands the ancient circular Tynwald Hill, 12 feet high and surrounded by four concentric steps or platforms. It is believed that the hill is atop an old burial mound that made it a place of Celtic gatherings where the Old Midsummer rites (July 5) were held during Pagan times.

From the chapel nearby, the queen's Lieutenant Governor leads the Tynwald's procession to the hill, on a path strewn with green rushes, a survival of offerings to the sea God, Manannan. Once at the hill, there is the reading of old laws as new ones are presented. As each new law is read, it is followed by loud shouts and cheers. This custom prevails today. Before the lieutenant governor can sign a law into effect, he must wait for the assent of the people.

6–13 July
Games to Honor Apollo

The games of Apollo originally took place on July 13, but, because of their popularity, they were gradually extended backward until, by the late Republic, they began on July 6. A Greek God, Apollo was first introduced to the Romans as a God of healing, oracles and prophecies, and hunting and music. Augustus regarded Apollo as his personal deity and built a temple to him in Rome next to his house on the Palatine Hill. It was here that the games to honor Apollo took place each year.

7 and 8 July
The Consualia and Festival of the Pales

It is believed that the festivals in honor of Consus were possibly to celebrate the harvest. Consus had an altar in the Circus Maximus in Rome that was kept underground. The altar was only exposed on July 7 and August 21, with burnt sacrifices offered in July by the *Sacredotes Publici* (state priests) and in August by the *Flamen Quirnalis* (priest of Consus) with the Vestal Virgins in attendance.

The Festival of Pales, held on *Nonae Caprotinae* (nones of the wild fig), was a feast of serving women held in honor of Juno Caprotina.

9–16 July
Panathenaea

The Panathenaea (all-Athens) was celebrated annually in Midsummer. Instituted by the Athenian tyrant Pisistratus in the mid-500s B.C., the festival served as a national religious holiday that celebrated the birthday of Athena—the city's patron Goddess. During the weeklong celebration, there were sacrifices, sports competitions, and a procession of citizens. Every fourth year the festival was especially elaborate and called the Great Panathenaea, during which the procession of citizens would carry a *new pelops*, or lady's gown, up to the Athenian Acropolis. The gown was then offered up to the ancient olive wood statue of Athena.

Athena

Athena the warrior Goddess was admired for her intelligence and dislike of senseless violence and was adept at the art of peace. The patroness of architects, sculptors, spinners, and weavers, Athena was the proctor of all towns, especially Athens, of which she was the patron deity. The most notably celibate of the Greek Goddesses, Athena's symbols include the owl, olive tree, spear, shield, chariot, and flute. Her colors are gold, blue, and olive green, and she is associated with the numbers 9 and 25.

10 and 11 July
Parade of Godiva

Up until the 1960s, the appearance of Lady Godiva, astride her white steed, was part of the procession held during the eight-day Midsummer Corpus Christi festival. Unfortunately, the rowdy behavior and vulgar humor of the occasion drew Victorian disapproval. The parade was reinstated in 1969 but toned down considerably.

Godiva, Lady of Coventry, was the wife of Earl Leofric and a devout and generous patron of the church. She was considered to be saintly and blessed of God. Godiva begged her husband to free Coventry from tax until, angry at her persistence, he told her that if she rode naked across the crowded marketplace he would grant her request. She agreed but allowed her hair to hang loose so that her whole body was veiled and only her legs exposed. Her husband considered this to be a miracle and lifted the tax.

12–16 July
Obon, Festival of the Dead

Celebrated in Japan, *Obon* or *Bon* may be compared with All Hallows' or All Souls' Day. It is commonly believed that the spirits of the dead return to earth during Obon, and preparations are made to receive and honor them. Family shrines are cleaned, and special meals known as the "Feast of Fortune" are prepared for the spirits. Because lanterns are lighted in the cemeteries and at doorways to welcome ghostly visits, the holiday is often called the Festival of Lanterns. Obon festivals are often sponsored by Buddhist religious congregations and are celebrated in Japan and in Japanese communities throughout the world.

13 July
Highland Games

The Highland Games gained great popularity with the patronage from Queen Victoria in 1848 and have continued ever since. The most spectacular event of the games is the opening march of kilted, bonneted, and sword-wielding clansmen, led by the chief of the local clan and followed by a show of bagpipers.

Athletic events usually include hurdle and running races; putting the stone (throwing the 56-pound weight); throwing the hammer (an iron ball on a chain); and, the most noteworthy of all challenges, tossing the caber (a 19-feet-long, 120-pound pole). More than 70 sets of Highland Games are currently held between Midsummer and September, most of which takes place in the Highlands.

14 July
Bastille Day

This patriotic holiday in France commemorates the seizure of the Bastille, a fortress in Paris that housed political prisoners such a Voltaire and the mysterious Man in the Iron Mask. It was the storming of the Bastille that brought the lower classes into the French Revolution.

In the United States, Bastille Day is still celebrated by descendants of French Canadians, especially in Kaplan, Louisiana, a small town about 75 miles southwest of Baton Rouge. The Bastille Day celebration is of such epic proportions that it requires a special committee to monitor its activities. The high point of the festivities is the annual Bastille Day Wine Glass Race. The contestants each pay $15 to race a sloped walkway while balancing trays of wine-filled glasses on one hand. The first-place winner receives a bottle of *Moet & Chandon* and a trip to New York; second place wins a trip to Boston; third, dinner for two a local restaurant.

15 July
Travectio Equitum/Rowana

In ancient Rome, this was the parade of the cavalry in front of the temple of Castor and Pollux, the great Twin Horsemen, to thank them for their part in the victory of Lake Regillus in 496 B.C. The parade consisted of 5,000 riders wearing purple togas with red stripes and decorated with olive garlands.

This day is sacred to the Goddess of the rowan tree, Rowana—patroness of the secret knowledge of runes. The wood of the rowan tree is used for making protection amulets, and the wood is especially efficacious when cut on this day.

16 July
Pilgrimage to Saut d' Eau Waterfall

On July 16th, the Catholic holy day dedicated to the Virgin Mary (the Haitian Erzulie Freda), pilgrims from all over Haiti arrive at the Waterfalls of Saut d' Eau near Ville Bonheur to bathe in the blessed waters. Along the way, they tie pink ribbons to the trees closest to the falls in honor of the Goddess. Offerings of food are left in hopes that Erzulie will bring good luck and charm to each participant.

Erzulie, or Ezile Freda, is the Goddess of love and is connected with all aspects of beauty. She adores flowers, jewelry, rich clothing, and fine perfumes. She is envisioned as a light-skinned mulatto and considered to be the epitome of charm. Colors for Erzulie are pink, yellow, and pale blue. Her symbols include a checkered heart and a white lamp. Her tree is the laurel, and her favorite foods include sweet cakes, pink champagne, and rice.

Magickal Activity
Charm Lamp

Items needed: Yellow paint; olive oil; a magnet; cane syrup; honey; jasmine flowers; a floating wick; a bowl made from one-half of a coconut shell, cleaned and sanded smooth.

Turn the coconut bowl over and paint the *Vé-Vé* (heart sigil; pictured) around the bottom of the bowl. Allow to dry. When the paint is dry, fill the bowl with ⅓ each of the liquid ingredients, beginning with the cane syrup, then the honey, and then the olive oil. Make your wish and drop the magnet into the bowl. Thread the loose wick through its metal holder, and float it on top of the oil along with the jasmine flowers. Speak your desire over the bowl, and light the wick. When the wick has completely burned out, take the still-filled bowl to the nearest lake or river along with seven pennies. Make your wish one more time, toss the bowl and pennies into the water, then turn and walk away. Do not look back.

17 July
Turtle Day

Snapping turtles weigh about 10 to 12 pounds and are generally active during Midsummer. It was around this time of the year in Churubusco, Indiana, that Gale Harris, a farmer, heard that a turtle the size of a tabletop lived in the lake on his property. While Harris was patching his roof with the help of his minister, the turtle was spotted at a distance. Upon a closer look, it appeared that the turtle was four to five feet wide and about six feet long—in short a monster! With significant effort, and help from his neighbors, Harris sought to capture the turtle.

It seems that Harris tried nets, grapples, homemade nets and pens, professional divers, and even a female turtle as a decoy. After articles appeared in local papers, crowds began to gather to watch the various efforts. But, the turtle who came to be known as Oscar always managed to escape unscathed. In 1950, the town needed to raise funds to build a new meeting hall and decided to exploit the fame of Oscar, the so-called *Beast of Busco,* as its main attraction. The festival was such a success that the Midsummer pattern for Turtle Day was set and continues today.

The Turtle

Because of its slow and deliberate movement, the turtle is regarded as intelligent and prudent. Its ability to reach very old age assures it great respect. In most African legends, the turtle always comes away victorious and is usually associated with the God of rain, because of its ability to live both on land and in the water.

---

18 July
Feast of Saint Thenew

According to legend, Thenew of Taneu was the daughter of a sixth-century prince of Lothian in southern Scotland. When she was found to be pregnant by a commoner, her father had her thrown from the summit of Traprain Law, but she slowly drifted down—floating like a bird. She was placed in a leather coracle and set adrift, only to have a school of fish push her ashore. Unharmed, she then gave birth to her baby and became the patron saint of parents and unwed mothers.

19 July
Adonia

July 19th celebrated the *Adonia,* in honor of Adonis, whose name means "my lord." Around 1000 B.C., Adonis replaced the earlier Greek vegetation Gods and was then espoused to the beautiful Aphrodite. It was on this day in ancient times that their marriage was celebrated with great jubilation and revelry.

Adonis was born from a tree into which his mother had been transformed. He was put into a box and given to Persephone, the Goddess of the Underworld, who agreed not to open the box. But she did open the box, and then would not let Adonis return to the earth. A conflict ensued, and Zeus finally stepped in to rectify the situation by proclaiming that Adonis would spend half of the year in the Underworld and the other half on the earthly plane.

Magickal Activity
Candle Love Spell

Items needed: Handwriting or photo of desired one; one red image candle; rose oil.

Begin by dressing (rubbing) the candle with the rose oil to empower it with your desire. As you do this chant the following:

> *Bring unto me,*
> *The love that I see.*
> *That he (she) shall requite,*
> *All my love from this night.*

Light the candle, and place it on top of the handwriting or picture. Allow the candle to burn for one hour, and then extinguish it. Each night for six consecutive nights repeat the spell, dressing the candle with the oil each time. On the last night of the spell, allow the candle to burn out. Carry the handwriting or picture with you the next time you plan to see the one you desire.

20 and 21 July
The Binding of the Wreaths

The Binding of the Wreaths is a popular festival among the young people of Lithuania. At sunset, the participants go into the forest and gather summer flowers. The flowers are then made into wreaths, crown circlets, and streamers to be exchanged the following day between lovers.

22 July
Concordia

The oldest and main temple of Concordia was built or restored to commemorate the end of the struggle between the patricians and the plebeians. Concordia was the personification of concord and was sometimes identified with Homonoia, the Greek embodiment of harmony. Her temple stood on the northwestern side of the *Forum Romanum* in Rome, at the foot of Capitoline Hill, and was the site of the annual festival held in her honor on July 22. As with most Roman festivals, there would have been games and a sacrifice. This is a good time to rekindle an old friendship or begin new ones.

23 July
Neptunalia

The Neptunalia venerates the divine God of the sea, Neptune. Originally a freshwater God, Neptune acquired his maritime status when he was identified with the Greek Poseidon. At Rome, there was a temple dedicated to Neptune in the circus *Flaminius* within the *Campus Martius* where his festivals were held on July 23 and December 1.

Neptune was one of only three Gods to whom a bull might be sacrificed (the others were Mars and Apollo). According to legend, he had a wife whose name was Salacia, Goddess of the salty sea and inland guardian of springs. It is believed that the Goddess Sulis, who is still worshiped at the sacred hot springs at Bath, may have been an aspect of Salacia.

> *Mighty Neptune, may it please,*
> *Thee, the Rector of the Seas.*
> *That my Barque may safely runne,*
> *Through thy watrie-region;*
> *And A Tunnie-fish shall be,*
> *Offer'd up, with thanks to thee.*
> —Robert Herrick,
> "To Neptune, Hesperides" (1648)

24–30 July
Cheyenne Frontier Days

This six-day annual event is the remnant of the old Mexican-American rodeo contests held in the American Southwest shortly after the Civil War. They flourished in Texas and by 1880 were nationally popularized by touring, circus-like extravaganzas such as Buffalo Bill Cody's "Wild West Show."

Established in 1897, Cheyenne Frontier Days has become an elaborate folk event and developed traditions of its own. For example, in 1987 the festival treated more than 30,000 hungry spectators to its free breakfast of pancakes, ham, and coffee. The batter for the more than 100,000 pancakes was mixed in a cement truck so that no one would have to wait in line for more than 20 minutes.

The food was prepared by the 390-member Cheyenne Kiwanis Club and included 3,600 pounds of pancake mix, 1,130 pounds of butter, 300 gallons of syrup, 2,800 pounds of ham, and 520 gallons of coffee. That year, people from more than 50 states and 20 foreign countries enjoyed breakfast during Frontier days. In addition to the great food, Frontier Days celebrates with old time rodeo contests that include trick-riding, roping, bronco-busting, and pony races.

25 July
Tenjin Festival

Dating back to 949 A.D. the Tenjin Festival held in Osaka, Japan, enables the people to purge themselves of sickness and ill health. Traditionally, each participant brings a sheet of paper into the shrine, where he or she will then make a paper doll. The doll is then rubbed over the body and then taken to the *Dojima River* and dropped in. It is believed that all sickness and ill health are transferred to the doll and dispelled with the discarding of the paper.

Magickal Activity
Simple Healing Spell

Items needed: One sheet of green construction paper; a black pen or marker; string; one green votive candle.

Draw a human shape on the sheet of paper using the black pen or marker. Cut the figure out as you would a paper doll, and write your name on one side of it. Rub the doll over your body and visualize your health problems being transferred to the doll. Bind the doll with the string as you chant:

> *As I bind my illness into thee,*
> *Let good health return to me.*

Light the green candle and place the doll next to it. When the green candle has completely burned out, take your doll to the nearest river and toss it upon the water. As your doll is consumed by the water, so your illness is washed away.

26 July
Festival of Sleipnir

For members of Norse traditions, July 26 honors *Sleipnir,* the mythical horse of Odin that represents time and permits him to ride between the worlds. In Asatru, the eight-legged steed takes Odin between the three worlds: from the upper one of the Gods (Asgard), through our own middle kingdom of Midgard, down into the underworld of the shades (Utgard). As the Norse God of war and poetry and conductor of the dead, Odin's ability to transcend the planes of consciousness is what allows him the ability to oversee the fate of humans, and Sleipnir serves as his magickal transportation.

27 and 28 July
Hopi Kachina Dances

Celebrated annually, the Hopi Kachina Dances commemorate the Kachina—supernatural beings that help insure the survival of the tribe. The Kachina are believed to be ancient  spirits that guide and protect the Hopi people. It is believed that the dances and accompanying religious ceremonies are what bring the rain that will heal the entire community. The ceremonies usually begin at sunrise and end at sunset, when it is believed the Kachina return to the realm of the spirit.

29 July
Feast of Thor

Thor, the Norse God of sky and thunder, has rulership over those aspects of life most important to sailors, farmers, and the poorer classes. Thor is considered to be the God of right orderliness and the regulator and enforcer of oaths. According to legend, he was the common man's God, a tireless eater, drinker, and fighter who was inclined toward mankind; even the slaves came under his protection. On this day, Thor would have been invoked to bring fertility to the flock and fields for an abundant harvest.

30 July–6 August
Swan-Upping

This weeklong festival is held on the River Thames, between Sunbury-on-Thames, Surrey, and Pangbourne, Berkshire.

Since the 14th century the swan, the largest and most impressive of British birds, has been on the badges of the English royal house. Regarded as a royal bird, all swans are guarded by the crown and considered the property of the monarch. The only exception to this rule is a certain number of Thames swans that have belonged to the London Guilds of the *Vintners* and the *Dyers,* who are the last survivors of the various bodies once entitled by royal grant to "swan rights" on the river.

From the days of the first Queen Elizabeth, the two groups have organized an "annual swan voyage" along the Thames at the time when the new broods of cygnets are about two months old. All of the swans that are encountered are "upped" from the water, and the adults are examined for the beak marks that distinguish the guilds swans from the unmarked royal birds, and the cygnets are marked according to their parentage and ownership. During the 17th and 18th centuries, when the Vintners and the Dyers still used flamboyant state barges, the "upping" was accompanied by captivating processions, elaborate ceremonies, and a good deal of feasting. Today, even though much of the pomp and circumstance surrounding the "upping" has ceased, it remains a sound tradition and colorful event.

August

Named after the first Roman emperor Augustus Caesar, August celebrates the bounty of Mother Nature, and the harvest of grain. The Anglo-Saxon name for August is *Weodmonath,* "vegetation month," and the Frankish called it *Aranmanoth,* "corn ears month."

August marks the end period of Summer growth, the ripening of grain, fruits, and vegetables. To our ancestors, who were in the fields from first light to nightfall, this was a month dedicated to long hours of hard work. In medieval times, August was considered the beginning of Autumn, when housewives would be looking to preserve and store food for the harsh Winter months to come.

Beginning with the festival of *Lunasa, Lammas,* or *Lughnasadh,* this eighth month of the year commemorates the first harvest and is sacred to the Lugh, Celtic God of wisdom, parallel to the Norse Odin. This is a time of gathering and celebration, a time to reflect after our labors and count up our achievements and focus on what still may be needed to produce a personal bountiful harvest.

Magickal Themes for August:

Reflecting, sacrificing, planning, celebrating

Magickal Correspondences:

Colors:	Gold, yellow, amber, green
Food:	Corn, apples, grain, cider, bread
Plants:	Heather, fenugreek, oats, corn
Stones:	Amber, topaz, diamond
Symbols:	Pentacle, broom, corn-husks
Full Moon:	Wort Moon

1 August

Lughnasa, Lughnasadh, Lammas

*There is sufficiency in the world for man's need
but not for man's greed.*
—Gandhi

The festival of Lughnasa, Lughnasadh, or Lammas (from the Old English *hlafmoesse*, meaning "loaf-mass") was "the feast of first fruits" held in celebration of the first loaves baked from the first grain harvested. The loaves were taken to the local church and blessed by the priest, who would then distribute the loaves among the congregation. It was believed that, by observing this custom, abundance was insured for the coming year.

There is very little historical evidence to confirm exactly what took place at Lughnasa because of calendar changes and lack of written documentation. However, it is believed that Lughnasa was celebrated around the first of August and was very likely a tribal gathering to mark the beginning of the harvest and Summer roundup of flocks. Many of the festivals such as Lughnasa that were popular in Europe during the Middle Ages and died out over time are now being reinvented to serve modern needs, especially within the framework of the Wiccan religion.

Corn and grain are predominate features of Lughnasa, as they symbolize both fertility and prosperity. In some Native American traditions, the golden ears of corn are seen as the offspring of the marriage between the sun and virgin earth (the Sky Father and the Earth Mother). Both the corn and the grain (like bread and wine) symbolize humankind's labor and the ability to sustain life.

In Wicca, we commemorate the sacrifice of the God, as the spirit of vegetation, that dies so all might live and eat. As we celebrate the joy of work well done, we take time to consider what else we can do to improve on our past accomplishments. (See Appendix A for Lughnasa ritual.)

Magickal Activities
Magickal Cornbread

¾ cup flour   3 tsp. baking powder
¾ cup milk   1 Tbs. sugar
½ tsp. salt   1½ cups yellow corn meal
1 egg   2 Tbs butter melted

Preheat a greased 9" x 9" baking pan at 425 degrees. While the pan is heating, mix all the ingredients together in a bowl. As you mix the ingredients chant: *Corn and grain bring joy and gain.* Pour the mixture into the pan and bake for 25 to 30 minutes. Serve hot with butter and honey.

Lughnasa Charm Necklace

Ideally these should be made from fresh fruits, seeds, nuts, and corn. Use a strong nylon thread and needle to string the fruit and nuts (shelled).

Decorate with red licorice whips and fresh mint leaves. The necklaces are then exchanged between loved ones. It is customary to try to eat the necklace while your partner or lover is wearing it.

Lughnasa Incense

¼ part grains of wheat   ¼ part rose petals
2 parts frankincense   2 parts myrrh
¼ part red poppy seeds   3 drops rose oil
2 drops cypress oil

Mix all ingredients in a bowl. Immediately place in an amber colored bottle and cap tightly. Label and use during harvest rites.

⬦⬦⬦

2 August
William Rufus and St. Sidwell's Day

The second day of August is set aside to remember the Norman king *William Rufus*, who was shot by Walter Tyrrell during a hunting accident in the new forest. Many people believe that Rufus was a divine victim who sacrificed his life for the love of the land and its people.

St. Sidwell's Day commemorates the saint who had a chapel and well at Exeter dedicated to her. It is said that she was  murdered on the instructions of her stepmother, who was jealous of her wealth and position. The stepmother hired killers to cut of Sidwell's head, and when they did apparently a spring gushed forth. A well was placed over the spring and the chapel built nearby.

3 August
Aomori Nebuta

Each year in Japan the festival of *Aomori Nebuta* commemorates the beginning of the harvest season. The celebration begins with a parade of bamboo effigies, with grotesquely painted faces that are used to frighten away the spirits of sleep. The rituals that follow are designed to keep the farmers awake for longer periods of time allowing them to complete their harvesting.

4, 5, and 6 August
Crow Fair

Each August, the Crow Fair becomes a bold statement of pride for all who participate in its activities, as well as for those who witness its myriad of magickal customs. An echo of the Sun Dance ceremonies annually held by the Plains Indians, the Crow Fair takes place on the banks of the Little Big Horn River. The fair is a combination of secret rites and public performances designed to unite the tribe and validate its traditions. The fair attracts Native Americans from all over North America. They come to compete in the *all-Indian* activities that include a rodeo, merchant tables of bead and basket work, a drum contest, and an elaborate pow-wow dance.

7 and 8 August
Festival of Hathor

In ancient Egypt, the inundation of the Nile began about this time. As the waters rose to feed the land, Hathor, the cow-headed Goddess was honored (as were other deities).

Festivals in Egypt celebrated both the rising of the sun as well as the rising of the moon. During the daylight hours, the statue of the deity being worshiped was taken from the temple and paraded before the people—the only time the public was allowed to view the Gods, as the inner sanctums of the temples were closed to all but the priesthood. As the sun set and the moon began to rise, the nocturnal rights began. Candles in glass containers and lamps of colored translucent stone were ignited and decorated the homes and temples along the Nile. When the moon reached its zenith, prayers and blessings would have been said to bring the celebration to a close.

Hathor: *House of the Face or House of Horus*

Hathor is the Egyptian sky Goddess, daughter of Ra by Nut and sometimes the wife and/or mother of Horus the Elder.

 Hathor was Egypt's Goddess of love, music, pleasure, and dancing. As the embodiment of the ultimate female, Hathor was the protector of all women and supervised women's toilet (makeup). Her symbols are the bronze mirror, girdle, lamp, and all seductive scents including rose, myrtle, and benzoin. The lynx, cow, and sparrow are under her protection.

9 August
Chinese Milky Way Festival

This festival celebrates love and the art of weaving, similar to the Weaving Festival of Japan (July 7). The myth follows the life of the Sun God's daughter, who falls in love with a humble herdsman one day while weaving. The two were married, and soon the Goddess forgot about her weaving. This indifference toward her craft angered the Sun God, who then banished the herdsman to the other side of the Milky Way. On August 9, the two star-struck lovers are allowed to meet at the silver river of the Milky Way. The rest of the year, the Goddess must attend to her weaving.

Magickal Activity
Spell to Rekindle Love

Items needed: A white birthday candle; one white or silver 8-inch taper candle; jasmine oil; white parchment paper; a small jar; silver cord.

Begin by chipping the wax away at the bottom of the candle so you have two wicks. Next, carve two stars onto one side of the candle. Carve your initials into one star and the initials of your loved one on the other star. Anoint the candle with the jasmine oil as you chant:

> *As the stars doth rise above*
> *I beckon forth the return of love.*

Lay the candle aside and write the name of your loved on the parchment paper. Place the jar on top of the paper. Light the birthday candle and drip the wax from it onto the top of the jar, and then affix the silver candle to the top of the jar so that it will permit it to burn from both ends. When the candle is solidly attached, light both ends as you chant:

> *Dark starry night, and candle light,*
> *End forever this loveless plight.*
> *Bring back my lover to me,*
> *For this I will so mote be!*

Stay with the candle until it burns out. Tie up the parchment paper into a small packet and place under your pillow. Keep it there until your loved one returns.

10 August
St. Lawrence's Day

St. Lawrence (Latin, *Laurentius*), one of the seven deacons of Rome and instructed by the city to prefect to surrender the church treasures, is said to have assembled the beggars who fed off its charity instead. For this insolence, he was sentenced to death by grilling over a slow fire. It is recounted that his face was surrounded by a beautiful glow and he gave a sweet smile while saying:

> *This side is toasted, so turn me, tyrant, eat and see*
> *whether raw or roasted I make the better meat.*

St. Lawrence, with his somewhat dark humor, is the patron saint of cooks and bakers.

11 and 12 August
Old Lammas Eve, Festival of Lights, St. Clair

In some areas of England, Old Lammas Eve is the date for fairs and "handfast marriages"—trial unions in which either party is free to end after a year without the social stigma of divorce. It was also around this time that the crop fields were thrown open for Winter grazing.

The ancient Egyptian festival in honor of the Goddess Isis and her search for Osiris is commemorated on this day by a Festival of Lights. With the advent of Christianity, this day became the feast of Saint Clair, patron of embroiderers.

12 August
Festival of Hercules Invictus

On this day in ancient Rome, sacrifice was made to Hercules Invictus at the Ara Maxima, the great altar near the Circus Maximus. The myth surrounding Hercules is far older than Rome itself, having been introduced after Hercules had slain the villain *Cacus,* who was ransacking Evander's kingdom on the banks of the Tiber. A man's God, Hercules was known for his appetites and was even more popular because he had actually been a man at one time. The merchants and generals of Rome paid for the feast  that followed the festival, and, in contrast to other similar rites, the entire offering was consumed, and there were no restrictions placed on the types of food that could be served.

13, 14, and 15 August
Festival of Diana

This was a great day of celebration for Diana, the Roman Goddess of wild nature. She was invoked to avert storms that could possibly ruin the crops or hinder the harvest. Her festival took place at her temple, said to have been founded by King Servius Tullius, whose mother had reputedly been a slave. After its establishment, the temple became an asylum for runaway slaves, and this day a holiday for all slaves of both sexes.

Diana, who was originally identified with the Greek Artemis, was regarded as a Goddess of hunting and of the moon.

She was considered to be a protector of women, particularly in childbirth. One of her sanctuaries was Lake Nemi, where her priest was an escaped slave who had to kill his predecessor in single combat to take office, and then guard his station against all would-be successors.

Under Christianity, Diana became the Goddess of the Witches, whom the 10th-century Cannon Espiscopi condemned for believing that they could ride with the Goddess at night. Associated with the constellation Ursa Major, Diana's legend is still alive today in Tuscany, where she is held as the original supreme Goddess and mother of Lucifer of Aradia. Diana's day is Monday; her colors are silver, white, and crystal; gems include clear quartz, moonstone, and pearl. Her magickal weapons are the bow and arrow, and all dogs are sacred to her.

15 August
Assumption of the Virgin Mary

This is the major feast of Mary in the Roman Catholic Church, the "Feast of Mary in Harvest" in the Irish Church, and the major feast of all churches that bear her name. As the Assumption is commonly depicted with Mary ascending through the clouds, she has become the patron of aircraft pilots and crew.

Formerly on this day, women were admitted to the Sistine Chapel between first and second vespers, being excluded the rest of the year lest they should disturb devotions with their chatter.

Prayer

Almighty, ever-living God, You raised to eternal glory the body and soul of the immaculate Virgin Mary, Mother of your Son. Grant that our minds may always be directed heavenward and that we may deserve to share in her glory. Amen.

16 August
Anniversary of Elvis Presley's Death

Elvis Aaron Presley was born on January 8, 1935, in Tupelo, Mississippi, to a truck driver and sewing-machine operator.

By his late teens, he was locally successful as a country singer, appearing at the Grand Ole Opry and on the Louisiana Hay-ride. His big break came in the mid-1950s with an RCA recording contract and appearances on the Ed Sullivan show. His unique style of country, gospel, and blues brought him one smash record after another. Elvis redefined rock 'n roll. A good looking and gifted performer, Elvis was pure gold with a series of movies that made him a fortune and such hits as "Don't Be Cruel," "I'm All Shook Up," and "Love Me Tender."

In 1977, at the age of 42, Elvis died of heart failure at his Graceland mansion in Memphis. Each year on this date, thousands of people still visit Graceland to pay honor to the "King." Elvis followers (and those who make money off his name) have given him all the trappings of a true folk hero and even created a pseudo-religious festival for him during this second week of August. To his fans, Elvis still lives on in his songs and to some is even a martyr of a modern world gone crazy.

17–24 August
Odin's Ordeal Begins

According to legend, Odin hung on the World Tree Yggdrasil for nine days, during which time he discovered the runes. In modern Asatru, this discovery is celebrated with a nine-day festival starting on August 17. To those who follow the Norse traditions, Odin is the chief deity and appears in many aspects, among them leader of the wild hunt, God of magick, chooser of the slain in battle, and the dispenser of gifts. As king of Aesir, he was the God of fertility and the last sheaf of wheat was left in offering to his horse. His magickal number was 9 (the days he endured initiation on the World Tree), his color is blue (as is his cloak), and the raven of the Valkyries who attend him are sacred.

Magickal Activity
Rune Magick

Items needed: One small square of blue paper; a silver marking pen; one blue candle; nine inches of silver cord.

On the blue square of paper inscribe the pictured rune with the silver pen.

Light the blue candle and place it on top of the rune. Hold your hands over the candle and visualize your psychic abilities increasing as you chant:

> *Let it be, that from this hour,*
> *I know the secrets of psychic power.*

Leave the candle to burn for three hours. Extinguish the candle. Fold the paper in half and bind with the silver cord. Place the packet with your runes or cards. Keep the packet near when reading for yourself or others.

❖

18 August
Eisteddfod

The *Eisteddfod* is an assembly of Welsh poets and musicians that compete for an "eisteddfa" or bardic chair. This traditional festival is so important that it is announced 13 months in advance. From as early as the sixth century, the bards of Wales—who were the harpers, genealogists, and soothsayers, as well as court poets and story-tellers—are reported engaging in embittered disputes. Their special status was recognized by law so that formal competitions were used to settle differences. It was at Cardigan in 1176 when the Lord Rhys presented chairs to the winning poet and best performers on the harp, pipe, and fiddle. The Eisteddfod became a way to rate bards and thus distinguish them from the non-bardic traveling ministrals or vagabonds. Overseen by modern Druids, the festival attracts thousands of people even today, and though many awards are given for a number of categories, the place of honor is still reserved for original poetry.

19 August
Vinalia Rustica

Held in ancient Rome, the Vinalia was intended to secure Jupiter's protection for the growing vines and was dedicated to the Goddess Venus. An agricultural festival, to celebrate the start of grape season and wine-making, the first grapes were broken off and offered by the *Flamen Dialis* to Jupiter and then to Venus. The wine made at this festival would be saved and then opened at the Vinalia Parilia, held on April 23.

Venus Incense	Jupiter Incense
1 tsp. rose petals	1 tsp. pine gum
¼ tsp. crushed myrtle leaves	¼ tsp. ground clove
¾ tsp. powdered benzoin	¼ tsp. ground nutmeg
7 drops rose oil	3 drops sage oil
1 drop Fruit of Life oil	¾ tsp. juniper berries

For best results, pulverize the dry ingredients in a small food processor or coffee grinder and then add the oil. Store in tightly sealed glass jars.

20 August
St. Bernard

St. Bernard was born to noble parents in Burgandy, France, in the castle of Fontaines near Dijon. In 1112, Bernard revived the then-failing Cistercian order by bringing 30 of his followers to Citeaux, where three years later he founded a new monastery. St. Bernard was highly influential in public affairs, obtaining recognition for the Knights Templar, helping Pope Innocent II triumph over Anacletus—the antipope. He was a zealous opponent of heretics but, unlike many of his colleagues, opposed the persecution of the Jews. He died on August 20, 1153.

21 August
Consualia

Held annually in Rome on August 21, Consualia was a celebration of the harvest held in honor of Consus. There would have been a sacrifice and offerings of the first fruits, followed by horse racing in the Circus Maximus. The horses and chariots would have been decorated in garland and paraded before the altar of Consus, which was kept underground and exposed only on August 21 and at the preceding celebration of Consualia and the Festival of The Pales.

Consus

Consus was the ancient Roman earth God of granary and was connected with the harvest and Autumn sowing. He had an underground barn and altar at the Circus Maximus, which was only uncovered at his twice-yearly festivals. Consus also had a temple on the Aventine Hill, and his sacrifical offerings consisted of first fruits. Consus was also identified with the Greek God Poseidon and with Neptune, presumably because of his association with horses. His symbols include the horse and chariot, cornucopia, all fruits, vegetables, and grain. His colors are gold, brown, and rust, and his numerical values are 7 and 21.

---

22 August
Red Horse Race

Held near Carnwath, the Red Horse Race is said to be the oldest surviving running race in Britain, and the only one whose terms are determined by royal charter. According to a grant made by King James IV to the third Lord of Somerville in 1508, the owners of the Barony of Carnwath must pay annually "one pair of horse containing half an English bluecloth…at the Feast of Saint John at midsummer to any person running quickly from the eastern end of the town of Carnwath to the cross called Cawlo Cross." The original distance was about three miles. The custom probably originated with the Lord of Carnwath's practice of training messengers to give warning of border raids. The race was always taken with profound enthusiasm because technically, a lapse in the race could incur forfeiture of the land. Today the race is still run, but has changed dramatically and is no longer a part of the midsummer rites, but part of the August Agricultural Show, and has been reduced down from three miles to one mile.

23 August
Vocanalia

Vulcan was the ancient Roman God of fire and smithcraft. He had his own Flamen, the *Flamen Vocanalis*.

Very little is known about his festival and worship, but he did have a temple on the Campus Martius. Mythologically, Vulcan was the father of the fire-breathing monster Cacus, and his two consorts were Maia and Hora—also worshiped during his festival.

24 August
Festival of Luna

Luna, the Roman Goddess of the moon, often identified with Selene, the Greek Goddess of the moon. Her temple was on the Aventine Hill, and there was another temple to Luna "Noctiluca" (Luna that shines by night) on the Palatine Hill. It was during Luna's festival that the cover was removed from the *mundus*—ritual pit. This allowed the spirits of the Underworld to roam free. Thus, all public business was forbidden. Her other festivals were held on August 28 and March 28, at which times the focal point was again the removal of the *mundus*. It is likely that all secular activities were ceased at these times so as not to disturb or anger the spirits, should they damage the crops or obstruct planting and harvest activities.

Magickal Activity
Full-Moon Blessing Rite

Items needed: A clear glass bowl; one bottle of spring water; silver paint; one sprig of jasmine; one moonstone; one white pillar candle; gardenia incense and oil.

Inscribe the symbol (pictured) on the out-side bottom of the bowl with the silver paint.

Set your altar or small table so the light of the full moon will shine directly on it. Fill the bowl with the spring water. Place the bowl and all the other items called for on the altar. Light the white pillar candle and say:

> *Lady I now invite thee here,*
> > *As the Mother of sacred Earth.*
> *Whose power is beyond compare,*
> > *When dreams are given birth.*

Hold the moonstone and sprig of jasmine in offering as you ask this blessing:

> *Lady of desire, reflection of light,*
> > *You are my motion, direction, and second sight.*
> *Mother of creation the original source,*
> > *You are potential, power, the ultimate force.*

> *Grandmother of time, wise one from above,*
> *I summon thee here with honor and love.*

Gently place the moonstone and sprig of jasmine in the water. Pick up the bowl and hold it in offering to the moon as you say:

> *I call the brilliant evening star,*
> *The Virgin of celestial light.*
> *The Gracious Goddess from afar,*
> *Great Mother of second sight.*
>
> *Glorious Queen of the twilight hour,*
> *Wise and vigilant protector.*
> *Thou whose silent power,*
> *Is regal and most splendor.*
>
> *I beckon thee to now descend,*
> *Great Mystery behind the veil.*
> *She who rises time and again,*
> *The keeper of the Grail.*

Set the bowl down. Anoint your forehead with a drop of the water. Allow the candle to burn for one hour and then extinguish it. Carefully place the bowl in a window where the light of the moon will continue to shine on it. Just before sunrise, remove the jasmine and stone. Pour the contents of the bowl into a bottle with a lid, and close tightly. Keep the moonstone with your other magickal tools. Take the jasmine to the nearest river or lake and toss it in the water as you make a wish. Use the moon water to anoint candles and other magickal objects.

25 August
Opiconsivia, Festival of Ops

On this day in ancient Rome, the festival of Opiconsivia was held in honor of Ops, the Goddess of abundance. She was associated with Saturn and the Greek Rhea. Her festival was overseen by the Vestal Virgins, who honored her as the *bringer of help*. It was the custom for all who attended her rituals to sit on the ground in order to absorb some of her qualities. Possibly, this festival was designed to give energy and fortitude to those who worked the harvest.

26 August
Birth of Krishna

In India, this day celebrates the birth of Krishna (the rebirth of Vishnu as Krishna). Hindu philosophy teaches that when the world is in need of guidance, Vishnu enters to lead the people. The observances begin at midnight and images of the baby Krishna are paraded among the people. All cry out the word *victory* to welcome back the God and celebrate his return to the people.

Krishna is the eighth avatar of Vishnu. He was the son of Devaki, sister of King Kamsa of Mathura. The king killed Devaki's children at birth because he was afraid one of them was going to assassinate him. But Devaki managed to secretly hide Krishna and his brother with a cowherd's family. When Krishna was fully grown, he returned to Mathura and killed Kamsa.

27 and 28 August
Volturnalia

This is the feast day of Volturnus, the Roman God of the river and change of seasons. The origin of the God is obscure, and most of this cult died out by the late republic. As a God of the seasons, he had his own priesthood and was regarded as the father of water (an important aspect of a bountiful harvest). Little is known of his origins other than he may have been equated with Eurus, the Greek God of the southwest wind.

29 August
Wine-Growers' Fête, Death of Augustus

During the 16th century in Vevey, France, a wine-growers guild was formed. Each year, until 1889, they held a festival to celebrate the ripening grape. The festival was attended by thousands of people and those from the noble houses. There was a parade that included an image of the Goddess Pales adorned in blue robes followed by an oxen and a procession of children dressed as shepherds. Next came Ceres, followed by carts of wheat, harvesters, and bakers. Lastly came the vintners, ushering in the new season of wine-making along with carts of the last year's bounty. The parade was followed by a community feast, a good deal of wine drinking, and partying into the wee hours of the night.

30 and 31 August
Preston Guild Merchants

The Preston Guild has been held at the end of August with unfailing regularity since 1562. The Guild was chartered by Henry II in 1179. In Preston, as in other chartered boroughs, the grant of a Guild Merchant gave the wealthier members of the community the freedom to choose their own government officials, administer their own justice, and maintain a tight control on local trade. Except during fairs, none but the Guild Freemen would buy or sell in the town. Everything in Preston was controlled by the Guild, even deciding who could or could not live in the town. As did most dictatorships, this one got out of control, and so every 20 years the Preston Fair was held to hold court and re-grant privileges. Because of the infrequency of the Fair, during the 1800s it was extended to six full weeks of hearty drinking and feasting. Today, the Preston Fair has curtailed much of its former bawdy activities but is still conducted on a grand scale. There are no less than nine processions, an evening torch parade, and a full calendar of dances, sports, concerts, and special exhibitions.

September

The month of September derives its name from the Latin word *septem* (the number seven) because in the *old* Roman calendar (that began with March), September was the seventh month. For the Irish, this is the month of *Mean Fohhair*, the Anglo-Saxon *Haligmonath* "holy month," and to the Franks, it was *Witumanoth,* "wood month," when wood was gathered for the coming winter months.

For those who work the land, September is a month of gathering and preparation—the end of the corn, oats, and barley harvest—and the beginning of the wine-making season. It is a season of work and reward, rejoicing and reverence. September is a month of celebrations. The most notable—the Autumnal Equinox, the Mabon of the Celtic tradition, the Alban Elfed of the Druids, and the Winter Finding of the Norse.

The old farmers and weather almanacs cite September for being a month of extremes, able to dry up wells and break down bridges. It is said "fair weather first day of September, fair for the month." Magickally, September is a time to give thanks for all our blessings and achievements and a time to project for the ability to protect what we have accomplished.

Magickal Themes for September:
Giving thanks, celebrating, harvesting, reflecting

Magickal Correspondences:

Colors:	Amber, orange, brown, deep gold
Food:	Apples, wine, bread, meat, all grains
Plants:	Cinnamon, clove, nutmeg, benzoin
Stones:	Agate, aventurine, chrysoprase
Symbols:	Corn dolly, cornucopia, sickle
Full Moon:	Barley Moon

1 September

Monotony is the awful reward of the careful.
—A. G. Buckham

*A life spent making mistakes is not only more honorable
but more useful than a life doing nothing.*
—George Bernard Shaw

The first of September was a time of celebration in ancient Rome and when Jupiter the Thunderer (Celtic Jupiter Taranis) was honored. Originally, Jupiter was a sky God who controlled the weather and so the harvest came under his rule. Unfortunately, little is known of some of the lesser festivals, other than their date of celebration and the deity being honored.

In Ghana, the first day of September is Odwira, a time for the people of the gold coast to pay tribute to their nation and rejoice in their beliefs and customs that date back to the early 1600s.

The Persian prophet Zoroaster was born on this day in the sixth century B.C. He was the founder of Zoroastrianism, a Persian religion that teaches that the universe is a creation of holy power and evil power—dualism—and that humanity is caught in between these two battling forces.

2 and 3 September
Last Corn Harvest, King's Baker's Fire

In rural Scotland and parts of England, this was the harvest of the last corn, and a superstitious time indeed. The last sheaf had to be cut in a certain manner by the youngest maiden or youngest lad on the farm. The sheaf was not allowed to touch the ground and had to be carried to the hearth in triumph. In Wales and England, the standing corn was plaited together, and all the reapers threw their sickles at it until one cut it down. However it was cut, the last sheaf was always dressed in women's clothes or plaited into a corn dolly.

On this day in 1666, a fire at the King's Baker's Shop was fanned into the *Great Fire of London*. The fire started in Pudding Lane and extended to Pie Corner and, despite the efforts of the workman to stop it, the fire burned for four days destroying more than 13,000 homes and gutting St. Paul's, Guildhall, and the Royal Exchange.

4 September
Horn Fair

The Charlton Horn Fair was one of London's most popular and longest-running fairs until it was discontinued in 1872.

The fair was famous for its fixation on "horns." During the fair's heyday, thousands of people from all over England flocked to the fair wearing, carrying, and displaying horns. Every sort of horn imaginable and everything made from horn was for sale.

The legend behind the fair relates how King John was out hunting on Shooter's Hill when he stopped to rest at the miller's house. The only person home was the miller's charming wife. It seems that the king and the young woman began kissing when the miller walked in and caught them. He drew his dagger, threatening to kill them both, but, when he realized who he was dealing with, decided on some other compensation instead. The king thus granted him all the land visible from the Charlton to the river beyond the Rotherhithe and the right to hold a fair each year. However, it seems that the miller's neighbors became jealous and renamed the river boundary "Cuckold's Point." Each year at the fair, the disgruntled neighbors would wear horns and horned helmets to the fair in a mocking gesture. In popular culture, the phrase "he wears the horns" was used to identify the cuckold husband. Later on, the fair was moved to October, and then disbanded.

5 September
Labor Day

Peter J. Maguire, leader of the Central Labor Union of New York, suggested that it might be a good idea to have a celebration honoring the American working man. Acting on his idea, more than 10,000 workers showed up to parade in Union Square, New York. After the parade, there were political speeches, picnics, and fireworks. Afterward, Labor Day became an annual event. September 5 had no traditional or historical significance. According to Maguire, it was simply convenient—midway between the Fourth of July and Thanksgiving. Labor Day is still with us 120 years after its inauguration. Even though its original theme of being a trade union holiday has diminished and its date moved to the first Monday of September, the day remains important. It marks the end of the vacation season, is a day for family reunions and picnics, and is the kick-off for Fall festivals.

6 and 7 September
Festival of Durga

Around this date, the Hindu religion celebrates the Festival of Durga and the waning light. As the days grow shorter and the darkness increases, the Goddess is petitioned to guard and protect goodness against the ever-growing evil that dwells in the shadows.

The Goddess Kali is called Durga—impenetrable like a mountain fortress. She is often depicted as an attractive woman, riding a fierce tiger and being of the same yellowish color as the animal she rides.

Magickal Activity
Hymn to Kali

On a small table or altar place three candles, one white, one red and one black. Light the white candle and say:

> *Thee who whispers, gentle yet strong,*
> *Thee for whom my soul doth long.*
> *By most men Thee are seldom seen,*
> *Yet you ever reign as Virgin, Mother, and Queen.*
> *Kali, Kali, Kali*

Light the red candle and continue:

> *Thee who knows, and Thee who steels,*
> *Thee who gives birth, thee who feels.*
> *Ye are Maha Kali, Mother to all,*
> *Pray Thee now, come as I call.*
> *Maha Kali, Maha Kali, Maha Kali*

Light the black candle and conclude:

> *Thee who suffers as all men die,*
> *Doth with her victim in love lie.*
> *Ye are Kali Ma, Crone of despair,*
> *With whom our endings all must share.*
> *Kali Ma, Kali Ma, Kali Ma*

> *I pray Thee, Dancer of eternal bliss,*
> *Bestow upon me Thy wondrous kiss.*

For Ye are the Creatress of heaven and earth,
Who to my soul and spirit gave given birth.
Hail to Thee, Kali, Maha Kali, Kali Ma

Allow the candles to burn for one hour and then extinguish. Repeat when you feel the need for the feminine power and wisdom of this Great Goddess.

8 September
Feast of the Blessed Virgin

It was more than 1900 years ago, in a little Galilean village of Nazareth, that a holy couple of the royal lineage of the House of David was blessed with a child. The child was called Mary, the chosen one of Adam's race destined to be the Mother of Jesus Christ—the Christian redeemer of humanity. The feast of September 8 in honor of the Blessed Virgin Mary originated at Jerusalem, as did the solemnity of August 15— the Assumption of Mary.

Invocation for the Virgin Mary

Our Lady's love is deep and wide,
To some her secrets are denied.
But we shall fearless still proceed,
To follow where she may lead.
She fills our hearts with hope and laughter,
That we shall not fear of what comes after.
Praise be to the Virgin, Mother,
and to the Queen of Heaven.

9 September
Chrysanthemum Day

The chrysanthemum has been cultivated in Japan for more than 2,000 years. A chrysanthemum with 16 petals, gathered around a red central disk, was even the central emblem on the Japanese flag, and for centuries the flower has been used in cooking and for wine-making. In China, the wine made from the chrysanthemum is believed to bring both wisdom and longevity.

10 September
Abbots Bromley Horn Dance

Annually, the Abbots Bromley in Staffordshire, England, is host to one of the most well-known living relics of Pagan ancestry, the horn dance. Ancient reindeer antlers are attached to poles and carried through the streets by dancers who simulate fighting between rutting stags. Following the procession of stags are Robin Hood and Maid Marion, along with jesters of all sorts and people in medieval costumes riding hobby horses.

11 September

9-11-2001 (9-1-1)

8:42 a.m. American Airlines flight 11, a Boeing 767 with 81 passengers, nine flight attendants, and two pilots, hijacked from Boston en route to Los Angeles, slammed into the north tower of the World Trade Center in New York.

9:00 a.m. United Airlines flight 175, a Boeing 767 heading for Los Angeles, carrying 58 passengers, four flight attendants, and two pilots, slammed into the south tower of the World Trade Center in New York.

9:43 a.m. American Airlines flight 77, a Boeing 757 leaving Dulles airport for Los Angeles with 58 passengers and six crew members, crashed into the Pentagon. A portion of the Pentagon collapsed 30 minutes later as a result of the crash.

10:29 a.m. United Airlines flight 93, a Boeing 757 taking of from Newark, New Jersey, heading for San Francisco, carrying 38 passengers, two pilots, and five attendants, crashes just north of Somerset County, Pennsylvania, outside Pittsburgh.

In less than two hours, the world changed forever. Thousands of people died, the economy was shattered, and the most powerful nation in the world was brought to a standstill, all because a few politically and religiously intolerant men didn't like the American lifestyle.

> *There is perhaps no phenomenon which contains so much destructive feeling as moral indignation which permits envy or hate to be acted out under the guise of virtue.*
> —Erich Fromm

In ancient Egypt this day was set aside to honor the queen and all her predecessors. The queen was both ruler and High Priestess, as well as an initiate of the inner mysteries and earthly representation of the Goddess Isis. As the representation of the Goddess, the queen had the authority to decree that this day be a time of celebration and tranquility.

Magickal Activity

Prayer for Peace

Items needed: One pastel blue candle; three yards of silver ribbon; lavender incense.

Use the silver ribbon to make a peace sign (pictured).

Place the blue candle in the center of the peace sign and light the incense. Take a few moments to meditate on what peace means to you and those you love. When you feel the time is right, light the candle and say this prayer:

> *Gracious Goddess fill my mind with peace,*
> *Let all sadness and foreboding cease.*
> *Descend to me from the heavens above,*
> *And fill my heart with understanding and love.*
> *Thou who creates now protects and guides,*
> *Blessed be the Goddess who from the past presides.*

Allow the candle to burn for one hour and repeat when you feel the need for peace.

❀❀❀

12 September
Pumpkin Festival

In France, the pumpkin festival draws people from far and wide to search the produce markets in search of *The Mother of all Pumpkins*. Once the great squash has been decided upon, it is decorated and placed upon a throne, where it is allowed to remain for a respectable period of time. At the conclusion of the festivities, the pumpkin is made into bread and soup and shared among those in attendance.

13 and 14 September
All Souls' Day/Festival of Jupiter Optimus Maximus

All Souls' Day in Egypt was a festive occasion. Held in honor of the Goddess Nephthys, Mistress of the Palace, it honored the spirits of the dead. There most certainly would have been a royal procession among the common people, followed by a public ritual and the Ceremony of Lighting the Fire. All the other activities would have taken place in the temple that was accessible only to the priesthood of Nephthys and the royal family.

Jupiter Optimus Maximus ("Jupiter Best and Greatest") is the supreme Roman God. He was worshiped above all other Gods. The Ludi Romani games took place in September, with a special festival on September 13. The farmers' harvested fields and orchards demanded little attention, the military campaigns would be coming to a close with the soldiers coming home, and the populace was in a serious mood for "fun." On the Ides of September 13, Jupiter received a sacrifice of a white ox in gratitude for an abundant harvest and successful battle. This would have been followed by notorious Coliseum games that somehow seem to eclipse the significant religious character of the Roman Empire.

Magickal Activity

Jupiter Prosperity Talisman

Items needed: The fourth pentacle of Jupiter (pictured); pine incense; clove oil; one orange candle; four $1 bills; a round box painted dark blue.

Begin by placing all the items on a small table or altar. Pick up the blue candle. Inscribe on it your name and the amount of money—be reasonable—you would like to have. Anoint the candle with the clove oil as you chant:

> *Success and prosperity come to me,*
> *This I will so mote it be.*

Place the candle in its holder and light it. Gaze into the flame and visualize your desire.

Pick up the Jupiter pentacle, hold it in both hands, and chant the following to energize it with your thoughts and feelings:

> *Honor, wealth, and prosperity,*
> *Are what this talisman shall bring to me.*

Place the talisman under the blue candle. Take down the circle and leave the candle to burn for two hours. Repeat this spell four consecutive times. Each time, anoint the candle and repeat all of the steps just as you did the first time. On the last day, place the talisman in the box along with the money. Redo the spell whenever you have need of money.

15 September
Birthday of the Moon

In Japan, the Birthday of the Moon is an annual event of great importance. To many Eastern cultures the moon represents the supreme feminine aspect (Yin) of the universe—Yang being the supreme masculine counterpart.

Legend has it that the emperor Ming Wong and his dedicated monk were strolling one night in the palace gardens. Ming, gazing upon the moon, questioned his friend as to what the moon was made of. Rather than trying to explain, he magickally transported Ming to the moon. The emperor was so overwhelmed by the experience that upon his return, he showered his people with gold. When questioned about the event, Ming Wong explained that the miracle had happened because it was the moon's birthday.

16 September
Rosh Hashana

Rosh Hashana, the Jewish New Year, is a time of new beginnings. On this day, the best clothes are worn and "Good Year" greetings are exchanged. Originally, this was a one-day festival and the Fast of Trumpets, at which the *shofar* was sounded. For the Jewish community this is a time of judg-ment, repentance, soul-searching, and also of augury for the coming year. This is an entirely public festival, in contrast to the domestic nature of most Jewish holidays. In earlier times, a ritual cleansing was enacted by casting one's sins into the waters. Today, when possible, Orthodox Jews still assemble near the water for this rite.

17 September
Hildegard of Bingen

Hildegard of Bingen, Abbess of Rupertsberg (1098–1179), was known as the "Sibyl of the Rhine." The 10th child of noble parents, Hildegard joined a monastery at age 8 and took the veil seven years later. A visionary from childhood, she wrote three mystical works, together with saints' lives and works on natural history and medicine, but is more famous for her poetry and musical works. Honored in many German churches, Hildegard was never canonized, even though many miracles have been reported from her tomb.

18 and 19 September
Laguna Indian San Jose Day

During the late Summer and early Fall, the southwestern part of the United States supports an array of fiestas that honor various Catholic saints and feature elaborate processions, markets, dancing, and entertainment. The Laguna festival honoring Saint Joseph is a prime example. The pueblo of Laguna, some 45 miles west of Albuquerque, New Mexico, was established in 1697. Soon after, a Catholic mission was built there and became the official site of the festival. The origins of the festival have been lost over time, but more than likely they revolved around the mission's patron Saint Joseph and the plentiful late Summer harvest. Today the festival still attracts thousands of people for the two-day celebration. The fiesta begins with a procession for Saint Joseph from the mission to the fairgrounds, which is followed by a noontime harvest and corn dance. After the official opening of the festival, the adults flock to the enormous market for the exchange of local products and food, while the children enjoy carnival rides and games. The fiesta concludes with demonstration dances performed by local Indian tribes and the return of the statue of Saint Joseph to the mission.

20–23 September
Autumn Equinox/Alban Elfed/Mabon

Named *Alban Elfed* by the Druids and *Mabon* by the Welsh, the Autumn Equinox marks the completion of the harvest. Once again, day and night stand in balance with equal hours of light and darkness. As do most celebrations held around this time of the year, the Autumn Equinox focuses on the harvest, the waning sun, and the onset of Winter. In the rural countryside, those who work the land come together to cut the last stalk of corn and sheaf of wheat. Following the gathering in of the last sheaf is Harvest Home, a huge supper or feast of roast beef, chicken, a stew of harvest vegetables, home-baked bread and cheese, and plenty of ale and cider. In Scotland, and parts of England, the man who cuts down the last sheaf is honored as lord and master of the harvest. The young woman who plaited the sheaf would be seated next to him and regarded as his consort.

In Wicca, the Autumn Equinox marks the waning of the year when the Goddess descends into the Underworld. As she withdraws, we see the decline of Nature and the onset of Winter. Now is the time we count up our blessings, give thanks for our bounty, and look within. As the God's shadowy presence begins to emerge, we remember what it took to achieve our goals and what is needed to maintain them. (See Appendix A for an Autumn Equinox ritual.)

Magickal Activities
The Corn Baba or Dolly

To make a Corn Baba, strip the off the husks from a dried ear of corn and soak them in water until pliable. Drain the strips on a paper towel and press flat with a warm iron. Take one strip and wrap around a cotton or foam ball to form the head.

Attach the head to the cob with tape or glue. Use several long strips to cover the head and body. Cut a narrow strip of husk for arms and roll into 7" length. Tie off at the ends with string. Attach to cob and then fashion dress from strips of corn husks as pictured. Finish off the doll using the silk or yellow yarn for hair. Embellish with colored ribbon, buttons, hat, and a basket.

Flaming Apples

Prepare one apple for each person. Use McIntosh or Winesap apples. Wash, core, and peel the skin down about ½ inch from top. Fill the center with brown sugar and butter. Top with cinnamon. Place the apples in a baking dish with about 1 inch of water. Bake the apples for 30 minutes in a 350 degree oven. Remove the apples to a warmed serving dish; pour heated cognac over each apple, ignite, and serve flaming.

24 September
Festival of Poets

This annual event takes place around this date in Japan. Poets come from all across Japan to visit the Imperial Palace, share their local legends, and compose verses. After the usual pleasantries, the guests are seated and served a cup of sake, after which each attendee is expected to create a verse pertaining to his or her visit. The poems are then read and the winner becomes the nation's poet laureate.

25 and 26 September
Old Holy Rood Day

Old Holy Rood Day, known as Mid-Autumn Day in the Highlands of Scotland, is traditionally the beginning of mating season for deer. It is believed that whatever the weather is like in Scotland this day will continue for 40 days thereafter.

This is also the traditional day for women and young maidens to gather St. Michael's carrots. The root vegetable had to be taken in a special way by digging a triangular hole (the shape of St. Michael's shield) with a three-pronged mattock. The carrots were then tied with three strands of red thread and presented to male visitors on Michaelmas Day. Forked roots were exceptionally lucky and a portent of marriage.

27 September
Torch Day

This was the fifth day of the Greater Eleusinian Mysteries. In the morning, participants assembled, left the city by way of the Sacred Gate, and marched along the Sacred Road to Eleusis, where the procession arrived by early evening. This fifth day of celebration was called Torch Day because, with the setting of the sun, all those gathered carried torches that were dedicated to Ceres, in commemoration of her travels and her lighting the torch on Mount Etna.

28 and 29 September
Eve of Michaelmas, Michaelmas

September 28, the eve of Michaelmas, was a time of preparation everywhere. In the Scottish Highlands, the Michaelmas lamb without blemish was killed and the Michaelmas cake prepared. The cake was made from all the grains harvested, butter, eggs, and sheep's milk. It was then marked with a cross and cooked on a stone heated by a fire of sacred wood—oak, rowan, and bramble wood.

The following day, September 29, was the feast of Michaelmas, a celebration for the Archangel, Captain of the Heavenly Hosts, who cast the devil out of Heaven and who is the patron saint of soldiers.

In the south of England, this was Quarter Day and a "settling day" when rents and bills were paid, and laborers went to hiring fairs to seek new and/or better employment. Many of these fairs, such as the Goose Fair at Nottingham, were and still are famous for the sale of geese, a favorite food served at Michaelmas supper.

The Archangel Michael:
Fiery Prince of Light and Champion of Humanity

The best known of the Archangels, Michael's name means "Who is as God"—a perfect reflection of divine light.

Michael is the Prince of Light, leading the forces of good to conquer the powers of darkness. It was Michael who rescued Daniel from the lion's den and, according to Christian mores, he antagonizes Satan by meeting with each soul at the moment of death and offering redemption.

Symbolically, Michael represents the golden lion. Transmuted and perfected energy, he is the dragon-slayer who wields a magickal sword that defeats evil and, as the angel of death and divine justice, he holds a pair of scales to weigh the merits of humanity.

30 September
Lakshimi Puja

Lakshimi, Goddess of good fortune and vegetation, was the daughter of Brahma-Prajapati and the wife of Vishnu. As the Empress of the Sea, she was the patron of the fisherman along the south coast and on the islands. Seated on a lotus throne, Lakshimi rises from the ocean waters, serenely smiling. Her annual festival celebrates her continual goodness and helps to ensure an abundant harvest.

October

The eighth month of the year on the *old* Roman calendar, October derives its name from the Latin *octo*, the number eight. The Anglo-Saxon name for October was *Winterfelleth,* meaning "Winter is coming." For the Frankish, it was *Windurmanoth,* meaning "vintage month," and in modern Asatrú, it is simply called *Hunting.*

October is a time of festivity as well as foreboding. It marks the height of the Autumn season and that period of ripeness and decay that heralds Winter. In the Pagan Celtic calendar, the end of the month was known as Samhain, "Summer's End," when fire festivals ushered in the Celtic New Year. Later Christianized as All Hallows' Eve or Hallowe'en, Samhain was, and still is, a celebration of the dead—a time of mystery, magick, and portent for the year to come.

October has always been noted for its odd weather and sometimes second summer in many regions. In the United States, this return of summer is called Indian Summer; in Sweden, it is called St. Bridget's Summer. In Italy, it's called The Summer of St. Teresa. Rain in October indicates rain in December, whereas a warm October will make a cold February.

Magickally, October is the time to rest and reevaluate your life and goals. It is a good time to clean house—to get rid of any negativity or opposition that may surround your achievements or hinder future progress.

Magickal Themes for October:

Resting, reevaluating, protecting

Magickal Correspondences:

Colors:	Black, wine-red, red
Food:	Beef, wine, pumpkin, turnip,
Plants:	Wormwood, mugwort, nightshade
Stones:	Spinel, kunzite
Symbols:	Cauldron, tombstone, broom, runes
Full Moon:	Blood Moon

1 October

We do not free ourselves from something by avoiding it,
but only by living through it.
—Cesare Pavase

The mind is always prone to believe what it wishes to be true.
—Heliodorus

In ancient Rome October 1 celebrated the festival of Fides, the Goddess who was the personification of good faith. She was the patron of verbal contracts and was portrayed as an old woman with white hair. Her cult was thought to be very ancient, dating to the time of King Numa, and her temple was the Capitoline Hill, where a sacrifice was made to her on this day.

2 October
Guardian Angels' Day

This pre-Christian Roman holiday is still celebrated in Spain and Europe. In early Rome, every man had his *Genius* and every woman her *Iuno*. When the church writers had a dispute over which angels guarded a person, the day became linked with the feast of St. Michael (Sept. 29). However, in 1670, the two days became separate, and Guardian Angels' Day was moved to October 2.

Genius (pl. geni), meaning "begetter," was a man's guardian spirit that also enabled him to beget children. For women the spirit was called *Iuno* (Juno). Each household also had a genius that was worshipped by the family members whose birthday coincided with that of the male head of the household. The genius was usually honored along with the household Lar, at the Lararium. So popular was the concept that it even extended to groups of people. Even the city itself had its own guardian genius.

Magickal Activity
Discover Your Guardian Angel

Items needed: A sheet of paper; frankincense joss stick and holder; one white candle; a pendulum.

Place the sheet of paper on a flat surface and inscribe the letters of the alphabet on it. Light the frankincense and the white candle. Hold a pendulum or crystal, on a chain, over the paper as you recite the following prayer:

> *Dear Divine Angel,*
>   *Through this candle flame*

> *Guide my hand*
>> *To spell your holy name.*

Allow the pendulum to swing freely so that it can spell out the name of your angel.

3 October
Feast of Dionysus

The Grecian God of wine and revelry was honored on this day in ancient Greece. The wine from the previous year was mixed with the new to celebrate the end of the harvest season—a time of rest for those who worked the fields.

Dionysus was the Greek God of vegetation, wine, and fertility. He brought civilization and viticulture to many countries and was widely worshiped, often with wild-ecstatic rituals and orgiastic dancing. Most of his festivals coincided with the harvest and Spring fertility rites.

4 October
Feast of St. Francis of Assisi

Francis of Assisi (1182–1226) is one of the most revered of the Christian saints. He was distinguished for his joyous piety, asceticism, and compassion that extended to all living creatures. Francis was the son of a prosperous merchant who had him disinherited because of his extravagant gifts to the poor. Soon after this, Francis began to minister to the lepers near Assisi and then rebuilt a ruined chapel for them. In 1209, he received papal permission to begin his own order and established the Franciscan order. He traveled extensively throughout France and Spain, where his compassion for Nature spread. One legend has him preaching a sermon to Sparrows at Alviano, and another tells of him saving bees from freezing to death. On this day, many Christian schools allow the students to bring their pets to class so they can be blessed by the resident priest.

5 October
Festival of Old Women, Mania

Annually on this day, the farm workers of Lithuania celebrate the Festival of Old Women (Nubaigai). The last sheaf of grain that is cut is dressed up as an old woman and honored as the Goddess of the harvest. Traditionally, there is a last fruits market with homemade bread, jams, and all types of freshly canned goods for sale. At the height of the day, there are games and sports for the young people to play. With the setting of the sun, there is a feast and a good deal of dancing and merriment into the wee hours of the night.

On this day the Roman Goddess Mania (regarded as the mother of the Lares and the Goddess of death) was honored. At this time, the Mundus, a subterranean ritual pit believed to lead to the Underworld, was opened. The cover of the pit was regarded as the Gate of Hell. When lifted, the spirits of the Underworld were allowed to wander the streets of Rome. To help keep the spirits at bay, small ugly images were hung as charms in offering to Mania.

6 October

St. Faith's Day

St. Faith of Foi, a virgin martyr, is said to have been grilled over a fire (later found to be untrue). Cakes were made in her honor. In northern England, they were used by young maidens to divine the identity of their future husbands.

On St. Faith's evening, three girls would join in making a cake of flour, salt, sugar, and pure spring water. The cake would be turned nine times as it baked, each girl turning the cake three times. The baked cake was then cut into three equal slices that were then cut into nine slivers. Each sliver was then passed through a wedding ring belonging to a woman who had been married for seven years. All of the slivers were then eaten while repeating:

> *O good Faith, be kind tonight,*
> > *And bring to me my heart's delight.*
> *Let me my future husband view,*
> > *And be my vision chaste and true.*

As soon as all of the cake had been eaten, the girls were to retire for the night. While sleeping, each girl would see the face of her future husband in her dream.

7 October
Kermesse

This unique festival dates back to 15th-century Germany. Traditionally, this weeklong celebration focused on the digging up of an effigy that had been buried the year before. The object was ritually unearthed and then mounted on a brightly decorated pole that was paraded through the streets to announce the beginning of the festival. The opening procession was followed by a week of games, feasting, and dancing. At the end of the festival, the participants would dress up in their mourning attire and rebury the effigy in its grave, where it would remain until the next Kermesse.

8 October
Chung Yeung Day

Chung Yeung Day, the Festival of High Places, is China's annual good luck festival commemorating the ancient Chinese scholar, Haun Ching. Legend has it that on the advice of a fortune-teller, Haun fled with his family and friends to the high hills, thus avoiding the plague of death that killed everyone in the village below. During this mid-Autumn celebration, the people take to the hills and fly special kites that are considered to be good omens that drive the evil spirits away.

9 October
Leif Ericson Day

Born in Iceland sometime before 1000 A.D., Leif Ericson was the son of a Norseman, Eric the Red, who discovered and colonized Greenland. Leif left Greenland for Norway, where he was converted to Christianity. King Olaf commissioned him to convert the Vikings to Christianity, but on his way from Norway to Greenland he was blown off course and reached the coast of North America instead. It is believed that Leif Ericson landed in North America in 1004 (488 years before Christopher Columbus). There is some speculation as to who exactly discovered North America. As a mark of respect for Leif Ericson and the Norse explorers, the Congress of the United States authorized the president to proclaim October 9 of each year as Leif Ericson Day.

10 October
Festival of Lights

In Brazil, October 10 begins the two-week celebration of the Festival of Lights. Each town or village has its own unique practices, but, in general, the festival begins with a parade of penance. This is followed by the lighting of torches, candles, hearth fires, and oil lamps to drive away the evil spirits of the darkness that create confusion and bring bad luck.

Magickal Activity

Candle Protection Spell

Items needed: One dark blue candle; patchouli oil; pine or sandalwood incense; salt; water.

Anoint the candle with the patchouli oil as you chant:

> *Candle of protection, power, and might,*
> > *Protect me from evil with your pure light.*

Light the candle and the incense. Anoint your forehead with the patchouli oil. Sprinkle some of the salt and water around the candle. Visualize all negative thoughts and vibrations fading away as you chant:

> *Let all of the elements now combine,*
> > *To protect my heart and my mind.*
> *Let darkness and evil now fade away,*
> > *So that only good shall come my way.*

Leave the candle to completely burn out. Repeat when necessary.

11, 12, and 13 October

Festival of Meditrinali, Festival of Fortuna Redux, Fontinalia

Little is known about the ancient Roman festival of Meditrinali, other than it was celebrated on this day and was in some way concerned with the new wine vintage. The festival was associated with Jupiter and with the Goddess Meditrina, apparently invented to explain the festival.

The festival of Fortuna Redux (Fortuna the home-bringer) is held in celebration of Augustus's reentry into Rome, at which time the Senate held a dedication of Fortuna Redux's altar. Her temple was built in the *Campus Martius* by the emperor Domitian to celebrate his military victories in Germany. Fortuna Redux is just one aspect of the great Goddess Fortuna, who was believed to be in charge of steering people's destinies.

Fontinalia is the festival of the God Fons. This ancient Roman festival was held in honor of the God of springs and fresh water. Flower garlands were thrown into the springs and placed around the tops of wells to appease the God and ask his continued blessing on the fresh water supply. These types of festivals have little meaning for most of us today, but to our ancestors fresh water and an abundant harvest were not luxury items, but rather essential to their survival. Whatever it took to assure their continuance was done and usually with lavish abandon.

14 October
Festival of the Penates

The Penates were Roman Gods of the store-cupboard and protectors of the household along with the Lares. They were the guardians of the pantry, and small statues of them were placed, along with those of the Lares, within each household. They were worshiped along with Vesta (Goddess of the hearth). Just as with the Lares, a portion of food from every family meal was set aside for them or tossed onto the hearth fire as a small offering for their continued protection. The festival held for them on this day was a state affair and was held in honor of the Roman *Penates Publici*—the Penates that presided over the city.

15 October
St. Theresa of Avila

St. Theresa of Avila, Spain, was born in 1515. At the age of 12 her mother died and her father placed her in a convent of Augustinian nuns. She became a nun in the Carmelite Convent of the Incarnation near Avila in November of 1534.

Inspired by the Holy Spirit, and acting under the direction of St. Peter of Alcantara, she undertook the superhuman task of reforming her Order and restoring its primitive observance. Before her death in 1582, 32 monasteries of the Reformed Rule had been established. Among them, 17 were convents of nuns.

St. Theresa wrote many books on Mystical Theology considered by Popes Gregory XV and Urban VII to be equal to those of a Doctor of the Church (an unprecedented achievement for a woman). Accordingly, in 1970, Pope Paul VI added her to the role of the Doctors of the Church.

16 and 17 October
Kan-name-Sai Cermony, Hengest, Buchmesse

Annually on this date, the Japanese Shinto ceremony of Kan-name-Sai or Good Tasting Event takes place. The rice from the first harvest is offered to the Imperial Ancestors, and the ancient Sun Goddess, Ama-terasu, is honored. In Asian countries, rice is the main source of nourishment, equal to that of wheat in Europe. In Japan, rice is the symbol of abundance and divine provision. It represents immortality, happiness, fertility, primordial purity, glory, solar power, knowledge, and happiness and fecundity, which is its significance when thrown over brides at weddings.

Rice Pudding

2 cups cooked basmati rice	½ cup sugar
4 eggs	2 Tbs. melted butter
2 cups soy milk	½ Tbs. lemon juice
½ cup raisins	

Butter a baking dish and preheat the oven to 350 degrees. Add the cooked rice to the baking dish. In a large bowl, beat the eggs until frothy. Add the remaining ingredients and mix thoroughly. Pour the mixture over the rice, combining well with a fork. Bake the pudding until set, approximately 40 to 50 minutes. Serves 6.

In modern Asatrú, the 17th of October is the feast day of Hengest, the Saxon general, who along with Horsa, in the fifth century C.E., began the Germanic settlement of eastern Britain, which eventually became England.

Buchmesse is held in Germany each year at this time and is the world's largest book fair for the publishing industry. More than 90 countries send exhibitors featuring their latest titles, with attendance reaching more than 200,000 people.

18 October
Crabapple Fair

Held annually in Egremont since it was chartered in 1267, the Crabapple Fair is one of Britain's oldest festivals. It is famous for a number of traditions, includ-ing the distribution of free crabapples from a lorry that tours the village soon after noon. In recent years, common eating apples have been thrown to the crowds instead of the formerly used wild crabs.

The fair begins at dawn, when a 30-foot-high greased pole is erected in the main street of town. In the past, the prize for anyone who could scale the pole (which is impossible without the help of a human ladder) was half a sheep's carcass at the top. Today, climbers work for a pound note instead. Other morning activities include children's games, a scrimmage for coopers, and street races.

In the afternoon, there are more games, wrestling, and terrier racing. The most unique events take place in the evening. The first competition is a pipe-smoking contest to see who can keep a pipe burning longest without relighting. There is a contest for the best sentimental and best hunting songs. The main attraction is the World Champion Gurning Competition. This odd (and very old) competition involves putting one's head through a horse collar and making the most grotesque face possible. The championship is usually won by the individual who can take out his teeth and curl his lower lip upwards touching the nose.

19 October
Armilustrium and Bettara-Ichi

In ancient Rome, October 19 was *Armilustrium*, the festival of purification of arms. Held in honor of the God Mars, the *salii* (priests of Mars) danced in a procession in a square called Armilustrium on the Aventine Hill. The Salii danced and sang with sacred shields and then purified the military arms. The sacred shields and weapons were then put in storage until the next year's military campaign.

Magickal Activity
Victory Talisman

Inscribe the fourth pentacle of Mars (pictured) on a piece of red construction paper to bring victory in war, to bring victory over all enemies, and to help overcome obstacles. As you inscribe the pentacle on the paper, chant the following:

> *Mighty God of victory,*
> *Lend me your power,*
> *That I shall prevail*
> *From this hour.*

Once the talisman has been charged with your energy you will want to place it in a red silk or cotton pouch along with a bloodstone, garnet, and pinch of basil. Carry it for victory and to overcome obstacles.

In Tokyo, each year at this time the annual fair of Bettara-Ichi (sticky-fair) is held around the sacred shrine of the God Ebisu. Merchants and craftspeople come from all over Japan to sell their good luck charms. The most popular item at the fair is a rope with sticky pickled radishes tied to it. It is believed that when the rope is waved in the air, it frightens away the evil spirits and ensnares good luck.

20 October

Colchester Oyster Ceremonies

Since 1196, when Richard I bestowed rights for the Colne Fishery near Colchester, business has been booming. Generations later, the same corporation still maintains control over the Fishery. Every September, the mayor and councillors open oyster-dredging season with great fanfare. A proclamation of 1256, declaring that *"from time beyond which memory runneth not to the contrary"* the rights have belonged to Colchester. The company then drinks a toast of gin and eats gingerbread, upon which the mayor lowers the first oyster-dredge, thus opening the season.

On October 20, the famous Oyster Feast in Colchester is held at Moot Hall. The festival was a well-established custom by the 17th century, coinciding with the St. Dennis Fair dating from 1319. More than 400 people, often including the royal family, attend the feast, at which it has been reported more than 12,000 oysters have been consumed. This event is still held today in Colchester, Essex.

Oyster Stew

32 oysters, shucked   ¾ cup cream
¾ cup clam juice   ½ tsp. celery salt
5 drops tabasco   6 Tbs. butter
Paprika to garnish

Combine cream, clam juice, celery salt, and tabasco in a sauce pan. Simmer over low heat. Do not boil. Bring water in the bottom of a double boiler to a boil. Reduce to a simmer. In the top part, melt butter and add the oysters, stirring with a wooden spoon to let them heat evenly until the edges curl. Pour the hot cream mixture into the oysters. Let the stew reach a simmer, do not boil. Ladle into four deep bowls and sprinkle with paprika. Serve immediately.

21 October

Feast of St. Ursula and Her 11,000 Virgins

St. Ursula is believed to have been a British princess who fled with her maiden companions to avoid an unwanted marriage. The Huns captured and martyred St. Ursula and her maidens at Cologne, where a cathedral was raised in their honor. The virgin company, whose number was greatly overstated from 11 to 11,000 by medieval folklore, are the patrons of girls' schools.

22 and 23 October
Hi Matsur

Hi Matsur is a Japanese festival of purification and is celebrated annually at this time. Beginning on the eve of the 22nd there are torchlight processions and parades through the streets in honor of the ancient Gods. The procession ends at a sacred shrine in Kurama, where it is believed that the ancient ones return to earth at the stroke of midnight. Prayers and invocations will be offered into the following day.

24 October
United Nations Day, Anthony Mary Claret

It was on this day in 1945 that the world peacekeeping organization known as the United Nations was formally established (Charter, 1954).

Anthony Mary Claret (1807–70) began the Missionary of the Immaculate Heart of Mary and later became the bishop of Santiago de Cuba. After narrowly escaping an assassination attempt by a gentleman whose mistress had been converted, Anthony fled to Spain, where he became confessor to Queen Isabella II and went into exile with her during the revolution of 1868. His contribution to education extended to the establishment of a natural history museum and school of language and music.

25 October
St. Crispin and St. Crispinian

This feast day honors two French Catholic brothers, Crispin and Crispinian, the patron saints of shoemakers. According to one legend, the two brothers were martyred by being pricked to death by a cobbler's awl. In another tale, they managed to survive four execution attempts because of their

devotion to the needy. And yet another tale has them beheaded. However, it is agreed that if one buys a new pair of shoes on St. Crispin day, he or she will have good fortune the rest of the year.

26 October
Ludi Victoriae Sullanae

The *Ludi Victoriae Sullanae* were the games held on October 26 to honor the Goddess Victoria. The festival was established in 81 B.C. to celebrate Sulla's victory over a large army of Sammites at the Porta Collina in Rome.

Victoria was the Goddess of victory, and her temple was on the Palatine Hill in Rome. She was the equivalent of the Greek Goddess Nike and was pictured with wings. Victoria was an important Goddess to the Romans, and she appears regularly on coinage from the late third century B.C. Victoria came to be regarded as the guardian of the empire, and her altar became a symbol of Paganism.

27 October
Allen Apple Day

In Cornwall England, Allen Apple Day was reserved for telling fortunes and divining one's true love. The unmarried men and women of Cornwall would pick an Allen apple. The apple would then be placed under the individual's pillow upon retiring for the night. Before dawn, the apple was retrieved and eaten. The individual would then go outside and stand beneath a tree. It was believed that the first person to pass him or her by would be his or her future spouse.

28 and 29 October
Festival of Fyribod, Saffron Rose Festival

In the Northern traditions, October 28 is the day of Fyribod, the day of foreboding upon which bad weather often heralds the onset of an early and extreme Winter.

At this time in Consuegra, Spain, the annual Saffron Rose Festival is held to honor the world's most expensive herb: saffron. Parades, folk dances, and markets add to the festive occasion. Dishes that have been enhanced with the delicate flavor of saffron are up for tasting, and the herb itself is sold.

Saffron (*crocus sativa*) is associated with love, the sun, and the God Eos. The delicate herb is added to love sachets and potions to bring about lustful feelings. In ancient Persia, pregnant women wore a ball of it near the stomach for a speedy delivery. When made into a tea, it is believed to promote one's clairvoyant abilities.

30 October
Punky Night

Around Hinton St. George, Somerset, just before Halloween, comes Punky Night. A punky—derived from pumpkin—is a hollowed-out mangold-wurzel, with shapes cut through the sides and a lighted candle placed inside of it to form a lantern. The local children paraded the streets with their punky lights and collect money as they chanted:

It's Punky Night tonight.
It's Punky Night tonight.
Give us a candle, give us a light,
It's Punky Night tonight.

The parade ends at the Victory Hall for the judging of the best pumpkin. After the best design has been picked, the Punky King and Queen are chosen—usually the two who have collected the most money for charity.

It seems that long ago, the menfolk of the village went to the Chiselborough Fair, where they got drunk off cider and could not find their way home. So their wives made punkies and set off together to gather them home. Since then, Punky Night has been an annual event.

31 October
Samhain, Halloween

Samhain (pronounced sow-in) marks the end of the agricultural season and the beginning of Winter. For the Celts, who inhabited the British Isles more than 1,000 years ago, Samhain was the beginning of the year and the cycle of seasons. It was a time when they turned to their Gods, seeking to understand the turning of the cycle of life and death. For the Celtic people, Samhain was a time when the gates between this world and the next were open. It was a time of communion with the spirits who were believed to roam free on this night. It was a time of divination, when the ancestors were contacted for warnings and guidance through the dark Winter months.

In medieval Ireland, Samhain was the major festival that marked the opening of Winter; it was sometimes spelled Samain or Samuin, although still pronounced the same. It was believed that Samhain was a time of unusual supernatural power, when all manner of fairies, goblins, and monsters roamed the earth.

It was unfavorable to walk about on this night, lest one might stumble onto an open fairy mound and fall victim to the fairy's enchantment.

Samhain was also a time of truce with no fighting, violence, or divorce allowed. Hence, it was a time of marriage. Accounts were closed, debts collected, contracts made, and servants hired. Magickally, Samhain is a time of reflection, ending things that are not producing results, and releasing negative thoughts. Samhain is the perfect time to make a talisman for self control and protection of the family and home. (See Appendix A for a Samhain ritual.)

Magickal Activities
Protection Charm

Items needed: One tsp. each of patchouli, sandalwood, and clove; an incense brazier; one self-igniting charcoal; a small white stone inscribed with the following protection sigil.

Place a piece of charcoal in your brazier and light it. Mix the herbs together, and sprinkle them over the glowing coal. As the mixture begins to burn, pass the stone through the smoke as you chant:

> *Within this stone,*
> *I pass my plight.*
> *Banished forever,*
> *From this night.*

Immediately take the stone to the nearest body of moving water. Toss the stone in and walk away.

Protection Incense

2 parts talcum base
2 parts patchouli
2 parts sandalwood

3 drops patchouli oil
3 drops sandalwood oil
3 drops sage oil

Mix all the ingredients together in a dark blue or black bottle. Label and cap tightly. Can be used during Samhain and for protection magick.

Witches Pumpkin Bread

1¼ cups all purpose flour
2 tsp. baking powder
½ tsp. baking soda
½ tsp. salt
½ tsp. ground cinnamon
¼ tsp. ground mace
⅛ tsp. ground cloves
¾ cup oat bran

1 cup pureed pumpkin
1 large egg
1 large egg white
¼ cup vegetable oil
¾ cup brown sugar
¼ cup orange juice
½ cup chopped nuts
1 small black stone

Preheat the oven to 350 degrees. Lightly grease a 9" x 5" x 3" loaf pan. Mix together the flour, baking powder, salt, cinnamon, mace, cloves, and oat bran in a large bowl.

In a medium bowl, stir together the pumpkin, egg, egg white, oil, sugar, and orange juice. Add this mixture to the dry ingredients and mix well. Fold in the chopped nuts. Add the stone as you chant:

> *Pumpkin bread on Samhain night,*
> *Makes our powers bold.*
> *As our minds and hearts take flight,*
> *We see what our futures hold.*

Pour the mixture into the loaf pan and bake for one hour or until an inserted toothpick comes out clean. Allow the bread to cool. Remove the bread from the pan and place on a serving board. Allow each person to cut a piece of bread. The one who gets the stone will place it in a glass of water next to his or her bed before retiring for the night. During his or her dreams, the spirit of a loved one will provide guidance for the coming year.

Protection for Your House

Items needed: A square of parchment paper; a black pen.

Print the following letters on the parchment with the black pen:

$$\begin{array}{ccccc}
S & A & T & O & R \\
A & R & E & P & O \\
T & E & N & E & T \\
O & P & E & R & A \\
R & O & T & A & S \\
\end{array}$$

Beneath the protective inscription, write the following:

> *Health to this house,*
> *Protected from all evil.*
> *Happiness on the hearth,*
> *Love for all within.*

Place the paper beneath the doormat at the main entrance to your home.

November

November is the ninth month on the old Roman calendar, the 11th month of the current Gregorian calendar, and the first month of Winter in the Celtic *Natural Year*.

The Anglo-Saxon name for November was *Blotmonath* (sacrifice month), for the time of year when the livestock were slaughtered, drained of blood, and salted for Winter food. For the Frankish, November was *Herbistmanoth* (Harvest Month). The Welsh called it *Tachwedd* (slaughter) and, for the Irish, November was *Samhain* (end of Summer).

In the rural household, November was a busy time. The animals had to be slaughtered and the meat prepared to last through the Winter. Absolutely nothing was wasted. The fat from the animals would have been rendered into lamp oil and candles, the feet boiled into useful jelly, and the intestines cleaned and used for sausage casings. Hams would have been put into brine, sausages hung in the chimney to cure, and the last of the root vegetables placed in the cellar for Winter use.

Magickally, the month of November is a time of transformation and release—a time to honor the darkness and meditate upon our achievements as well as our failures. It is a time of rest and reevaluation.

Magickal Themes for November:
Resting, meditating, releasing

Magickal Correspondences:
Colors:	Black, brown, red
Food:	Stew, sausage, pork, root vegetables
Plants:	Rosemary, sage, bay
Stones:	Tourmalated quartz, topaz
Symbols:	Hearth, broom, cauldron
Full Moon:	Snow Moon

1 and 2 November
All Saints' Day/ All Hallows' Day

*All men should strive to learn before they die
what they are running from, and to, and why.*
—James Thurber

*Youth had only spring green tones; we others of the more
advanced season, have a thousand shades,
one more beautiful than the other.*
—Count De Bussy-Rabutin

All Saints' or All Hallows' Day, according to Pagan custom, begins as the sun sets the evening before on Samhain, the festival of the dead. It was made into a celebration of all the known saints and martyrs of the Catholic Church in the seventh century. Originally, it was celebrated on May 13, but was shifted to this date in the eighth century to coincide with the Ppagan festival of the dead. This is a time of intercession for the dead souls that have not yet been purified and ascended to heaven. Family members and relatives send prayers for their loved ones in the hope of helping them. Mumming, bonfires, the decoration of graves, and fortune-telling games are associated with the celebration.

3 November
St. Martin

St. Martin de Porres was born in Lima, Peru, in 1579. At the age of 15, he became a laybrother at the Dominican Friary at Lima, where he spent his entire life. He worked as a barber, farm laborer, and nurse. He had a great desire to go on a foreign mission and thus earn martyrdom. Because this was not possible, he devoted himself to endless and severe penances. In turn, God endowed him with many graces and wondrous gifts. He also showed great love for animals and maintained an animal hospital for cats and dogs.

In the religion of Santería, St. Martin is one of the saints associated with Eleggua—the God of crossroads, opener of doors, and the divine messenger. Eleggua has mischievous tendencies but is good humored. He is the master of lies and the arbiter of truth. He is identified with Fate, the unknown, and unexpected changes. Eleggua, along with Oggun, Ochosi, and Osun, is given during the initiation of The Warriors (Los Guerreros). Eleggua's colors are red and black, and he is represented by a small cement head that sits in a clay dish behind the front door of his owner's home.

Magickal Activity
Ebbó (spell) to Attract Money

Items needed: One loadstone; a sprig of rosemary; a sprig of rue; a silver coin; anise; sweet basil; a piece of red cloth; red and black thread; a small piece of brown paper bag.

Place the loadstone in a dish. Place the rosemary and rue on top of the loadstone in the shape of a cross. Sprinkle with the anise and sweet basil. Chant the following over the dish:

> *Cash and coin is what I see,*
> *Coming in bundles straight to me.*

Lay out the cloth. On the brown paper, write your name and put it on the cloth along with the silver coin. On top of the cloth carefully set the loadstone with the herbs. Pull up the corners of the cloth to form a pouch, and tie with the red and black thread. The packet must then be buried near a bank on a Monday night as close to the full moon as possible.

4 November
Ludi Plebii

Ludi Plebii (Plebian Games) were held from the 4th to the 17th of November to honor Jupiter. The games included chariot racing and entertainment in the Circus Maximus. It is believed that the games were established around 220 B.C. by Gaius Flaminus when he was the censor. The only games that were more important than the Ludi Plebii were the Ludi Romani that were held during September, again in honor of Jupiter.

5 November
Guy Fawkes Night

Guy Fawkes Night is one of the most widespread and thriving of all the British holidays and one that was decreed by an act of Parliament. It was in the early hours of November 5, 1605, that Guy Fawkes was arrested. He had hidden 36 barrels of gunpowder in the cellar of Parliament and planned to blow it up that day, an act that would have wiped out the entire government of England—clearing the way for a Roman Catholic coup.

There are several theories, one of which claims that the gunpowder plot was covertly encouraged by an administration anxious to discredit its Catholic opponents. Whatever the truth, the act sparked a nationwide explosion of patriotism and Protestant enthusiasm. The commemoration has become a night replete with bonfires, beer-drinking, fireworks, and bands of children begging for money. Topping off the evening's festivities, effigies of Guy Fawkes are tossed onto the bonfires.

6 November
Tiamat, St. Leonard

In ancient Babylonian culture this day was celebrated as the birth of Tiamat, the primordial sea Goddess (the salt water), who with her consort Apsu (the sweet waters) created the world. According to mythology it was Tiamat that brought forth the heaven and the earth. Sometimes she is pictured as a dragon or serpent—the unconscious in its most primitive state.

St. Leonard's cult developed around the 11th century, when he refused to become a bishop and instead opted for being a simple monk. He was the patron of women in childbirth, having helped the queen when no one else was around. But he is most famous for his patronage of prisoners, especially those unjustly accused and bound in chains. Numbers of stories have been told of shackled prisoners that upon praying to St. Leonard found their chains broken.

7 and 8 November
Sadie Hawkins Day, Festival of the Kitchen Goddess

From the 1930s comic strip, the character Sadie Hawkins overstepped the boundaries of propriety when she asked a man for a date. And, though we have come a long way since those days of male domination, many still feel that it is the man's place to do the asking. So, on this day many schools and social organizations reverse the role and make it ladies' choice.

In Japan, November 8 is set aside to honor the Goddess Uke-Mochi-No-Kami—she who possesses food—and the kitchen Gods Oki-Tsu-Hiko and Oki-Tsu-Hime. The God of the kitchen range Kamado-no-Kami is also greatly honored and venerated in most households. On this day, all the pots and pans are washed, and offerings of rice and rice wine are left in honor of the hearth side deities.

9 November
Loy Krathog, Lord Mayor's Day

Loy Krathog is the traditional wishing festival of Thailand. On this day, small boats are fashioned from banana peels and lotus leaves. When the sun sets, people take their boats to the shore, where they fill them with offerings of incense and gardenia petals. A white candle is then placed in the boat along with a wish. The boats are then set adrift on the water. It is believed that if the candle in the boat stays lit until its owner can no longer see, then the wish will be granted.

After the calendar reform of 1752 the Lord Mayor's Day was moved from October 28 to November 9. It is on this day that "Mock Mayors" are elected in many of the poorer English towns. The elections are designed to poke good-natured fun at some of the more prestigious municipalities and their some-times pompous politicians. Of course, the more offensive the candidate is, the more joy in having him take the podium, whereupon a cabbage stalk is presented to him to serve as his mayoral mace. The festivities are usually followed by somewhat raucous behavior and of course the usual drinking and feasting.

10 November

Martinmas Eve,
Celebration of the Goddess of Reason

The old Pagan festival of Nincnevin, later Martinmas Eve, honored the Goddess Diana and her entourage. At Martinmas, the Germans celebrate this time by feasting on wild geese and then using the breast bone of the last goose to predict the weather for the coming months. It is believed that if the breast bone be fair and clear when the flesh has been eaten off it, the weather will be cold and full of hard frosts. However, if the breast bone is dark then the winter will be full of rain, snow, and sleet but warmer overall.

During the French Revolution, this day was celebrated with a parade through the streets of Paris. A young woman was chosen to represent the Goddess, and led the processional to the cathedral of Notre Dame, considered a center of learning, whereupon she was presented with a crown of oak leaves. It was hoped that the festivities would make the people aware of the importance of learning.

11 and 12 November
Lunantshees

This day has been set aside to honor the Fairy, an important element in most Irish folklore and mythology. For the Irish, the Fairy is believed to be the decedent of the small, dark, Neolithic people who invaded early Europe. Being small and dark and living close to the land allowed them to quickly hide from their enemies. This ability, along with their elusive mannerisms, led people to believe they were capable of magick, shape-shifting, and invisibility.

Magickal Activity
Fairy Dust

Grind the following herbs into a fine powder:

1 Tbs. woodruff	1 Tbs. clover
1 Tbs. rose petals	1 Tbs. jasmine
1 Tbs. meadowsweet	

Place the powder in a dark blue jar. Inscribe the following symbol on the jar:

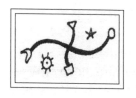

Hold the jar tightly against your heart as you chant nine times:

Nature spirits and Fairy friends,
Bless this dust to serve my ends.
I place my trust and faith in thee,
To bring me love, wealth, and prosperity.

Lightly dust the bed with the powder to increase passion and love. Place some of the powder near the threshold of a business to attract new customers, and sprinkle some around the perimeter of your home to create an atmosphere of happiness and good will.

13 November
Juno—The Feronia

Feronia was a Goddess of spring flowers and woods (also associated with Flora) and, although this day was named for her, it became a day of recognition for Juno, Minerva, and Jupiter. The celebration took place on the Capitoline Hill where all three were enshrined. Juno was the sister-wife of Jupiter, forming a triad with Minerva. The festival would have included an animal sacrifice and an evening torch light processional.

14 November
Dyfrig (Dubricius), Feast of Musicians

Dyfrig was the son of a princess whose father was so angry at her pregnancy that he ordered her thrown into the river Wye. When she did not drown, he ordered her burned at the stake.

However, it seems that her executioners were negligent, and she gave birth before they could carry out their assignment. The baby was then presented to the king, whereupon the child preformed his first miracle and cured his grandfather of leprosy. Later, Dyfrig became the abbot of Caldey Island and, as the Archbishop of Caerleon, presided at Silchester at the coronation of the 15-year-old Arthur.

This day also celebrates the Druidic Feast of Musicians and honors the Celtic Gods of music. It is the custom for Wiccans and Pagans to gather around the bonfire for an evening of song and story-telling. The festivities are usually brought to a close with everyone writing out a wish and then tossing it onto the fire. During inclement weather, the fireplace and hearth provide a warm and welcome alternative.

Magickal Activity

Fireplace Magick

Items needed: One square of red paper; a piece of yellow paper ribbon (for each person doing the spell); a small bottle of heliotrope oil; a jar of basil.

Light a fire in the fireplace. Have each participant write out his or her wish on the square of red paper. In the center of the square, place a drop of the heliotrope oil and a pinch of basil. Fold the paper into a packet and secure with the yellow ribbon.

Each person will then silently speak his or her wish and toss the packet into the fire. The group will then chant the following as the packets are consumed:

Blazing fire, burning bright,
Make my wish come true this night.

15 and 16 November
Dewali (Festival of Lights)

It is around this time of year that *Dewali*, Hindu Festival of Lights, ushers in the new year. Hinduism is considered to be one of the oldest living religions. It was not founded but rather evolved over a period of 4,000 years. The religion is made up of many sects, and beliefs include the doctrine of Karma, as well as the worship of numerous Gods and Goddesses considered to be forms of the one Supreme Being.

The word *dewali* means cluster of lights, and the illumination of lamps, bonfires, and fireworks all play an important part in the weeklong festival. The devotees of Vishnu hold that this was the day he killed the demon, but the most popular belief is that Dewali celebrates the coronation of Rama, a manifestation of Vishnu, following his conquest of the demon ruler of Sri Lanka, Ravana. During Dewali, effigies of Ravana are burned, merchants settle the past year's accounts, games of chance are played, and presents are given.

17 November
Western Lights

This is the third, and last, of the festivals of the dead in China. Clothing, money, and other gifts are burned in honor of the ancestors and loved ones. Candles, special foods, and rice wine are placed before personal shrines to fortify them during their journey through the spirit world.

18 November
St. Elizabeth

St. Elizabeth was born in Hungary in 1207, the daughter of Alexander II, King of Hungary. At the age of 4, she was sent for her education to the court of the *Landgrave of Thuringia,* to whose infant son she had been betrothed. As she grew in age, her piety increased. In 1221 she married Louis of Thuringia, and, despite her high position, she led an austere lifestyle and devoted her time to charitable works.

Louis was religiously inclined and much admired his wife's virtue. They lived an exemplary life and had three children when tragedy struck: Louis was killed fighting the Crusades. Heartbroken, Elizabeth fostered her children and in 1228 renounced the world. She built the Franciscan hospital at Marburg and devoted herself to caring for the sick. She died at the age of 24 in 1231.

19 November
Night-Fowling, Makahiki

According to the Perpetual Almanack of Folklore and *Markham Hunger's Prevention 1621*, this is the best time for night-fowling. The weather should be mild and the moon full. One is to then take a small bell with a melodic sound, a net, and a bundle of straw into some stubble field. The net is then to be laid upon the ground close to the bushes. The bell is then tolled to awaken the fowl lingering nearby. A fire is then started with the straw to frighten the awakened birds out of the bushes and into the net.

Makahiki is the beginning of the Hawaiian harvest season when the Pleiades become visible in the night sky. According to Greek legend, the Pleiades were the seven daughters of Atlas and the Oceanid Pleione; sisters of Hyades. Zeus placed them in the heavens to help them escape the amorous inclinations of Orion, who had fallen in love with them.

20 November
Deadman's Day, Feast of St. Edmund

Edmund, like William Rufus, reigns among those who have been herald as divine victims—the king slain for the love of the land and his people. Edmund was the king of East Angles in 865. In 869, he was captured by the Vikings, who offered to spare his life were he to share his kingdom with their leader, *Ingvarr the Bonless*. Edmund refused to relinquish any of his land or people to the heathen leader. Thus, Edmund was tied to a tree and used for target practice for the Danish archers, after which he was beheaded. Following his ritualistic death, his head was thrown into a thicket. When his followers hap-pened upon it they found a grey wolf guarding the head. His tomb, in the holy city of Saint Edmundsbury, has been the site of many miracles, and it was upon his bones that the barons swore their oath that led to the Magna Carter—the begin-ning of human rights in England.

21 November
Festival of Kukulcan

It was on this day that the ancient Mayan people paid hom-age to the God Kukulcan. His name means "the feathered snake whose path is the waters." Later merged with Quetzalcoatl (Plumed Serpent) he was the great God of wisdom, wind, and fertility—the inventor of agriculture and the calendar. He was identified with Venus as the morning star and portrayed as a feathered serpent and sometimes as a bearded man. The Mayan religion permeated all aspects of life. Their festivals were times of great celebration and focused on seasonal changes and agriculture. Generally, their festivals included games, feasting, dancing, and human sacrifice.

22 November
Ydalir

For those involved with Nordic traditions, this day is Ydalir, the Valley of the Yews, and falls under the rulership of Ull (Uller, Ullur, Ullr). Ull is the Norse God of Wintertime, skiing, archery, and hunting. His name means "Brilliant One" and he is invoked during duels. He is the son of the Earth Mother Sif and an unknown father. Ull has been associated with Aurora Borealis and with the oath-ring; vows on the oath-ring were sworn to him. Even though he is seldom mentioned in myth and legend, his cult was widespread in ancient Scandinavian countries.

23 November
St. Clement

St. Clement, the patron of blacksmiths and an aspect of the Norse wizard Wayland Smith, is honored on this day. Apparently of Jewish origin, he is traditionally considered as the third pope after St. Peter. Additionally, St. Clement was the patron of hatters. While fleeing from his prosecutors, his feet became blistered, and to ease the discomfort he placed wool between his feet and sandals. From the perspiration and pressure of his feet the wool became compressed and assumed a uniformly compact substance, which has since been designated as felt. In Rome it is said that he improved on the product to produce felt for hatters. On this day most Catholic countries, especially Ireland, hold festivals in his honor.

24 November
Thanksgiving (approximately)

The American Thanksgiving Day began in Plymouth Colony, Massachusetts, in 1621, and celebrated the Pilgrims' first year's harvest. Originally set by president Abraham Lincoln as the last Thursday of November, the holiday was changed by Franklin D. Roosevelt in 1939 to the fourth Thursday of November.

Actually, days of thanksgiving are far older than our American celebration, which is an adaption of Lammas (Loaf Mass Day). In Britain, it was celebrated on August 1, when the wheat crop was good. In fact, most agricultural peoples have special days set aside to celebrate a good crop and the end of the harvest—usually referred to as the Harvest Home. Our modern Thanksgiving is a combination of two very different customs: the harvest home feast and a formal day of thanksgiving proclaimed by community leaders to celebrate a victory. It was during the Revolutionary War that the need for national holidays, rather than local holidays, developed. It was George Washington that first declared November 1, as a national day of thanksgiving. But regional traditions were too strong and the day never caught on. With the Industrial Revolution and hundreds of immigrants pouring into America, the need for a national day of thanksgiving was once more addressed. It was finally during the Civil War that President Lincoln, in an effort to unite the country, declared the last Thursday of November as Thanksgiving Day. The holiday began with the usual morning church service, followed by a feast and then games.

Today we celebrate Thanksgiving with parades, the largest being Macy's New York display, which began in 1927 with the appearance of Macy's huge balloons designed by puppeteer Tony Sarg. The construction of the balloons is carefully executed by the Goodyear Aerospace Corporation, in Akron, Ohio. Preparations for the parade are yearround, reaching a peak the day before Thanksgiving when the balloons arrive at 77th Street and Central Park West. They are removed from their crates and anchored with sand bags and giant nets. On Thanksgiving Day, more than 2000 of Macy's employees arrive at 6 a.m. to march in the parade, which, 75 years later, is still the highlight of Thanksgiving Day.

25 November
Chinese Harvest Moon Festival,
St. Catherine's Day

It is around this time of the year that the Chinese celebrate their Harvest Moon Festival. According to Chinese belief, the moon influences the crops and is therefore held in high esteem, especially when it is full. The chief symbol of the Moon Festival is the "moon cake," a small cake made in the shape of a moon. The cake is about an inch thick and filled with sweetened soy bean paste, whole egg yolks, and melon seeds. The cake is baked to a golden brown and served with *pomelo*, which is similar to a grapefruit except twice as large and very sweet.

Unlike a lot of Chinese festivals, which are preceded by days of preparation and often followed by days of recovery, the Moon Festival only lasts one day. Along with the moon cake, small figures of rabbits and other small animals are made into cookies and placed in small reed cages. The use of the rabbits has special significance. According to Chinese mythology, a rabbit lives in the moon, forever busy pounding out the elixir of life.

St. Catherine was one of the major female saints of the Middle Ages, always portrayed with the spiked wheel on which she was to have been broken, but which itself was broken by a thunderbolt from heaven. According to her legend, she was a virgin of noble birth and exceptional intelligence who bested 50 philosophers in a debate ordered by the emperor. She was known as Catherine of the Wheel and the patron of spinsters. On her day in France, women have the right to ask men to marry.

Magickal Activity
Marriage Proposal Spell
Items needed: A small table or altar covered with a green cloth; one green 7-day knob candle; rose oil; a Venus pentacle (pictured); a picture of your loved one.

Begin this spell on a Friday night during the waxing moon. Etch your name on the top knob and your lover's name on the last or bottom knob of the candle. Anoint the candle with the rose oil as you chant:

> (Name), *your thoughts are just of me,*
> *No other face but mine you see.*
> *For as this spell I do fashion,*
> *To fill your heart with love and passion.*

Place the picture face-up on the table with the Venus pentacle on top of it. Set the candle on the pentacle. As you light the first knob chant the following:

> *I kindle within the flame of desire,*
> *The proposal of marriage to inspire.*

Leave the candle to burn until the first knob has been consumed. At the same time each night repeat the spell exactly as you did it the first time. On the final night you must stay with the candle until the last knob has burned out but not scorched the pentacle or picture. Carry the pentacle and picture with you when you next meet your loved one.

26 and 27 November
Gujeswari Jatra, Senegal Initiation Rites

On this date the Goddess Gujeswari Jatra is honored by the Hindus and Buddhists of Nepal. Activities fill the day beginning with prayers to the Goddess. These are usually followed by a musical procession through the streets where participants sing sacred songs to praise Gujeswari. The activities come to a close after sunset with more prayers and songs that are usually followed by a fast until the following evening.

It is around this time of the year in the Basari villages of Senegal that the young men are initiated into manhood. The elaborate rituals take months of preparation that test both the minds and bodies of the candidates. The initiates then compete against each other in village games to demonstrate their courage and masculine strength. The festivities are brought to a close with a feast and dance.

28 November
Last Chance Day

This was considered to be the last chance to marry before the beginning of Advent, during which marriage was frowned upon. It was believed that if a man wanted to marry a women who was in debt, he would not be responsible for the woman's financial obligations if he took her, dressed only in her under-garments, from the hands of a priest.

29 November
Stir-Up-Sunday

Stir up we beseech thee, O Lord, the wills of the faithful people: that they plenteously bringing forth the fruit of good works.

This passage is the beginning of the Church of England collect for the Sunday before Advent.

It was also on this day that Christmas pudding was ceremonially made. All the family had to take a turn stirring the mixture in a clockwise direction while making a wish. Afterward, the mother or senior woman of the household would hide a coin, a thimble, and a ring in the pudding, symbolizing wealth, a single life, and impending marriage, respectively.

30 November
Saint Andrew's Day

Saint Andrew, one of the first of Christ's 12 apostles, was in fact a Galilean fisherman and the brother of Saint Peter. He is the patron saint of Scotland, where during the fourth century, some of his bones were brought to what is now Saint Andrew's in Fife, and, since medieval times, the X-shaped saltire cross upon which he was supposedly crucified has been the Scottish national symbol. In both Russia and Scotland, Andrew is the patron of fishers and fishmongers. Although once celebrated to a riotous extent, the day is now met with little regard except for those who gather for the traditional supper of singed sheep's head, haggis, and lots of whiskey.

December

Decomber was the 10th month on the old Roman calendar, named after *decem*, Latin for 10, and *Decima*, the middle Goddess of the three Fates. In Asatru, the Gregorian month of December is Wolf Moon, the Frankish called it *Heilagmanoth* (Holy Month), and for the Irish it was *Mi na Nollang* (Christmas Month).

Since antiquity, the month of December has seen the birth of many solar saviors and dying Gods. These include Osiris, the Syrian Baal, Adonis, Apollo, Helios, Mithras, and Jesus. It is the host month for the Winter Solstice (also called Yule, Alban Arthuan, and Midwinter) and Christmas, the major festival observed by contemporary society.

For the Scottish, December 31 is Hogmanay and commemorates the solar divinity *Hogmagog* or *Gogmagog,* a solar giant represented by a chalk-cut hill figure at Wandlebury, close to Cambridge. For the ancient Romans, December was the month of Saturnalia, a weeklong festival to honor Saturn, the God of seed sowing. For most of us, the 31st is New Year's Eve, a time of celebration and joy. Magickally, December is a turning point, a time to remember the past as we plan for the future. It is a month of joy, celebrations, and rebirth and a time of cold, barren earth, and darkness.

Magickal Themes for December:

Celebration, rebirth, remembrance, planning

Magickal Correspondences:

Colors: Red, gold, silver, white
Food: Plum pudding, gingerbread, goose, beef
Plants: Mistletoe, bayberry, poinsettia, pine
Stones: Hematite, sugilite
Symbols: Yule log, Yule tree, stang
Full Moon: Oak Moon

1 and 2 December

Festivals of Neptune and Pietas

Mediocrity knows nothing higher than itself,
but talent instantly recognizes genius.
—Sir Arthur Conan Doyle

You do ill if you praise, but worse if you censure,
what you do not rightly understand.
—Leonardo Da Vinci

December 1 celebrated the festivals of Neptune and Pietas. This festival was the equivalent to the one that was held on July 23 at the temple dedicated to Neptune in the *Circus Flaminus* within the *Campus Martius*. There would have been games, a sacrifice, and, more than likely, some sort of horse and chariot race.

Pieta, a Roman Goddess who was the personification of respectful duty, is often portrayed in human form and sometimes accompanied by a stork, the symbol of deferential duty. She was frequently represented on coins, which were considered to be a symbol of the reigning emperor's virtues. Her temple was in the *Circus Flaminius* and later at the *Forum Holitorium*, where her December 1 festival was held.

It was on the 1st of December in 1750 that seven men (for a wager) buttoned themselves into the waistcoat of Mr. Edward Bright of Maldon, Essex, who had expired at the age of 29 and was considered to be the fattest man that ever lived in Britain.

On December 2, Tibetan Buddhists make their annual pilgrimage to the world's oldest tree in what it known as *Bodh Gaya*. The tree was planted in 282 B.C. and is believed to be an offshoot of the *Bodhi* tree—the tree that the Buddha sat under when he attained enlightenment.

3 December
Bona Dea

On this day in Ancient Rome, the fertility Goddess, Bona Dea, was once again honored (see 3 and 4 May). In myth, Bona Dea was the wife of Faunus and excelled in the domestic arts.

Her temple was on the Aventine Hill, but her rites were conducted by the Vestal Virgins in the home of the leading magistrate, under the supervision of his wife. Men were strictly forbidden from attending or witnessing these rituals. Little is known of exactly what took place, but wine (called milk) and honey were blessed, possibly to be used later in fertility rites.

4 December
St. Barbara, Chango

Saint Barbara was the beautiful daughter of a wealthy noble-man named Dioscorus, who had her shut in a tower to discourage the attentions of her numerous suitors. Upon discovering that she had become a Christian, he attempted to have her killed, but she miraculously transported out of his reach. Dioscorus then denounced her to authorities, who submitted her to torture. When she refused to give up her religious convictions, he ordered her killed and beheaded her with his own sword. At once, thunder struck and a lightning bolt from heaven fell, striking him dead. This is the source of St. Barbara's power over thunder and lightning and her direct link with the Santería God of lightning, *Chango*. In this Afro-Cuban religion, the Orishas (Yoruba Gods and Goddesses), were synchronized with Catholic Saints and worshipped.

One of the most popular Gods in the Yoruba pantheon, Chango is the embodiment of passion, virility, and raw power. He is envisioned as a noble, courageous, and incorrigible womanizer. A bit of a rake, but nonetheless charming and forever loveable and generous. His colors are red and white. His symbols are the tower, lightning bolt, double-headed ax (usually covered with red and white beads), and a wooden bowl, known as a *batea*.

Magickal Activity
Chango's Wishing Apple
Items needed: One red apple-shaped candle (available in import and craft-supply stores); one 6-inch

square piece of parchment paper; a small red cotton cloth bag; a red pen or marker; a pin or needle.

Place all the items on a small table. Using the red pen write out your wish on the piece of parchment paper. Take the pin or needle and etch your name and wish on the apple candle. Set the candle on top of the parchment paper and light it as you chant:

God of lightning, thunder, and fire
Grant my wish, manifest my desire.

Leave the candle to burn for one hour and then extinguish. Repeat daily until the candle has completely burned out. Wrap whatever is left of the burned candle in the parchment paper, and place in the red bag. Bury the bag beneath the largest tree in your yard or a nearby park. Leave six pennies near the tree as an offering for Chango.

5 and 6 December
Walt Disney's Birthday, St. Nicholas's Day

It was on December 5, 1901, that the legendary Walt Disney was born. During his life, his magickal imagination inspired and uplifted the hearts of people all over the world. Walt's Disneyland was the product of a dream he had one night, and Disney World his crowning achievement. His Florida theme park is truly a kingdom, complete with its own police force, fire departments, transportation systems, and major Disney highways and hotels. And who says magick doesn't work?

Today, Advent begins on the fourth Sunday before Christmas and heralds the coming of Christ. In the past, Advent began on December 6, St. Nicholas's Day. Very little is known of Nicholas, who was the bishop of Myra in Turkey, but he was very popular in the Middle Ages. One legend tells how he revived three small boys that an innkeeper had murdered and salted down so he could make them into pies, and another tells how he threw three bags of gold through the window of a poor man's house so his daughters would have dowries. St. Nicholas is linked with children, and in England on this night they receive presents in  his honor. This was also the date on which "Boy Bishops" were chosen by the Church to oversee the choir and rule over the Christmas celebrations.

7 December
La Quema del Diablo

In Guatemala, as part of the Advent season, people bundle up their old belongings and garbage, which is then ritually burned to ward off evil spirits. It is believed that by doing this the people will be purified and live longer.

During Victorian times, this day was dedicated to the evergreen rosemary—the rose of the Virgin Mary and special plant of Christmas. It was believed that the plant blossomed on Christmas Eve and acquired its scent from the garments of the infant Jesus. In English households, the plant is picked on this day and dried for winter potions and potpourris. There was an old saying, "where rosemary grows, the woman rules the house."

8 and 9 December
Ama-terasu

At this time of the year, the ancient and most important of all the Shinto divinities, Ama-terasu, is honored. Ama-terasu is the daughter of Izanagi and Izanami, the Gods of creation, who gave birth to the islands of Japan. So bright and great was her luster, Ama-terasu was sent to heaven to govern humanity. Later she was joined by her brother Tsuki-Yumi, the Moon God. Ama-terasu is the supreme deity of all the ordinary people and of the royal family. The Emperor is descended from her grandson and is the high priest of her cult.

10 December
Lux Mundi, Liberty

December 10 was the Roman feast of *Lux Mundi*, the Light of the World. It was also on this day in 1793 that the French actress *Mille Maillard* was selected to personify the Goddess of Liberty. She was brought to Notre Dame and seated on the altar, where she was handed a lighted candle to signify liberty and the Light of the World.

According to the *Five Hundred Points of Good Husbandry* (Tusser, 1573), this was the time that proper folk lay in stocks of firewood and made jumble-biscuits.

The 17th-century *Fairfax Household Book* reveals:

> *To make the jumble-biscuits, take twelve yolks of eggs and five whites, a pound of sugar, half a pound of butter, three-quarters of an ounce of mace finely beaten, a little salt, half an ounce of aniseeds, and half an ounce of caraway seeds. Mix all of this together with as much flour as will work it up into paste, and so mold it into rings or knots. Bake the biscuits until hard and serve forth with spiced wine.*

11 December
Blowing the Midwinter Horn, Agonalia

The Netherlands festival of *Blowing the Midwinter Horn* is more that 2,000 years old and takes place annually on this date. All around the countryside, farmers take out their birch-wood horns and blow them. It is hoped that the sounds emanating from the horns will frighten away any evil influence that may effect the settle upon the land during the Winter season.

Agonalia, called *dies agonales*, was held four times a year in ancient Rome, possibly for Janus, although even the Romans seemed to be unsure exactly which deities were actually involved. However, at each of the celebrations a ram was sacrificed at the Regia and a different God honored, including Janus, Vediovis, and Sol Indiges.

12 December
Sada, Tonantzin, Our Lady of Guadalupe

Annually on this day in Iran, huge bonfires are ignited as the sun sets to exemplify how the power of light can overcome the power of darkness. As the fires burn, the evil influences that linger among the shadows of darkness are dispelled, thus allowing people to overcome obstacles and reach their fullest potential in the seasons to come.

It was on the hill of Tepeyac, just north of Mexico City, in 1531, that an Indian named Juan Diego saw an apparition he believed to be the Virgin Mary. The vision instructed him to have a church built on the spot, which had formerly been the cult-site of the Aztec Mother Goddess Tonantzin. At the time, the bishop disbelieved him, until the Virgin appeared for a third time and miraculously produced roses that Juan Diego presented to the bishop. As he did, the portrait of the Virgin appeared on Juan's cloak. The shrine was built and is still a famous place of pilgrimage.

13 December
St. Lucy

St. Lucy, born in Syracuse, Sicily, claimed her Christianity at an early age, giving away all her goods and refusing the suitor chosen by her parents. Enraged, they had her eyes torn out, but they were miraculously restored before she was put to death. Her cult was important from early times, and in Syracuse her martyrdom is annually celebrated with a great procession in which her bier is carried through the streets.

Under the old calendar hers became the longest night. Because light returns after her day in Sweden, she is patroness of harvest and light; all threshing, spinning, and weaving must be done before her day. Although Swedish calendars still hold with a daily saint, hers is the only day celebrated. The churches are full, and everyone dresses in white and sings songs in her honor. One girl is chosen to represent St. Lucy and bedecked with a red sash and a crown of lighted candles. Her female attendants wear silver sashes and silver crowns; the boys wear pointed white capes and carry silver stars in their hands. The religious processional is followed by a feast of saffron buns, ginger biscuits, and *glögg* (hot spiced wine). Her feast day marks the beginning of the 12 days of Christmas.

Magickal Activity
Candle Friendship Spell

Items needed: Rose oil; rose incense; a photograph of the person(s) you want to work the spell on; a pink candle for each person; a needle.

Inscribe each person's name on a candle with the needle and anoint with the rose oil. Place the candle(s) along with the photographs on a small table, covered with a pink cloth. As you light the candle(s), chant the following:

> *Friendship is a gift the Gods bestow,*
> > *It lives through heat, rain, and snow.*
> *With this candle I form the bond,*
> > *That will endure this life and beyond.*

Allow the candle(s) to burn out. Carry the pictures in your purse or wallet the next time you plan to meet with your friend(s).

14 December
Nostradamus

It was on this day in 1503 that the famous astrologer-prophet Nostradamus (Michel de Notre-Dame) was born. From an early age, he experienced many psychic visions that eventually led him to study magick, astrology, mathematics, and the Qabalah. It was around 1555 that his first collection of predictions was published, followed by a second and much larger edition of his now-celebrated rhymed quatrains. Even after his death in 1566, his works remain the prototype of predictive astrology.

15 and 16 December
Halcyon, Sophia

In ancient Greece, December 15 began the Halcyon Days— the seven days before and the seven days after the Winter Solstice. It was during this time that the sea was calm and the kingfisher, a magickal bird and symbol of the Goddess Alcyon, could lay her eggs. Legend has that it was the bird nesting upon the waters that made them calm, thus creating an atmosphere of peace and tranquility.

December 16 is dedicated to the Goddess Sophia. According to Hebrew philosophy, Sophia is the personification of wisdom, the inner wisdom that functions of itself. Many Greek churches were dedicated to Sophia, and, in the Sistine Chapel's painting of God reaching out a finger to touch Adam, she appears behind God. A Gnostic Aeon, Sophia was so filled with the desire to generate out of herself, without a spouse, that she gave birth to the whole cosmos, including a daughter Sophia Akhamoth, who in turn began to generate, but on a lower and denser plane. It is Sophia Akhamoth who brings wisdom to humankind.

17–23 December
Saturnalia

Out of all the ancient Roman festivals this was the most beloved. The festival grew out of the dedication-day of a temple to Saturnus, the God of seed and sowing. It is also equated with the Greek Kronos, father of Zeus, and supreme God during the age of the Golden Race. It was believed that Saturn had been the king of Italy in a time of equality and abundance.

The festival began with a sacrifice at the Temple of Saturn, which was followed by a great public banquet. During the Saturnalia, all shops and schools were closed, and gambling—usually prohibited—was allowed. Each household chose a mock king to preside over the festivities, masters waited on their slaves, presents were given, and the entire household celebrated. Many of the time-honored traditions and customs of Saturnalia were absorbed into the later Christian Christmas that fell on December 25.

18 December

Festival of Epona, Mesa de Gallo

This was another of the festivals dedicated to the Celtic horse Goddess, Epona. Her worship was most popular in eastern Gaul and on the German frontier. So popular was Epona that she was honored with festivals in Rome, which was unique for a Gaulish deity. Epona was sometimes associated with the Celtic Mother Goddesses, and in Germany she was portrayed as a triple Mother Goddess.

An annual festival in the Philippines, Mesa de Gallo begins at sunrise when the people take to the streets with every imaginable noisemaker in existence. The parades of people clanking, banging, and hooting are believed to frighten away the evil spirits that may linger and thus affect future crops and harvest.

Magickal Activity

Change Your Luck Spell

Items needed: One black-cat candle; patchouli oil; a mirror.

Anoint the black-cat candle with the oil. As you do this, visualize your luck changing and good things coming to you. Place the cat candle on the mirror (reflective side up). Light the candle and chant:

> *Black cat power,*
> *From this hour,*
> *Reflect the light,*
> *Make things right.*

Leave the candle to burn for one hour. Repeat this spell every night, at the same time, until the candle has been consumed. Discard any wax left and put the mirror away.

19, 20, and 21 December

Winter Solstice, Midwinter

The Solstice, taken from the Latin for "the Sun stands still," is considered to be the *true* New Year—astronomically as well as spiritually. At this time, we see the simultaneous death and rebirth of the Sun-God, represented in the shortest day and longest night of the year. From this time forward, the sun grows in strength and power as the hours of daylight increase.

Midwinter, or Winter Solstice, marked the end of the first half of the Celtic year. As was Samhain, which has the Roman festival of Pomona and the Christian All Souls grafted on to it, the Celtic Winter Solstice was subsequently confused with the Roman Saturnalia, and later the Christian Christmas. Mythologically, most of the Midwinter celebrations focused on the symbology of a new or younger God, overthrowing the older or father God, which would then bring forth a new and more potent life to the people and the land.

Although the Solstice takes place on December 21, Midwinter (renamed Yule by the Anglo Saxons) covers several weeks on either side of the Solstice. In medieval times, Yule began around St. Nicholas's Day and ran until Candlemas. Eventually, Yule was redefined to mean either the Nativity (December 25) or the 12 days of celebration beginning on this date. The word *Christmas* then replaced Yule in most English-speaking countries. However, the Danish preserved Yule as a way of maintaining their old style of festivities that incorporated several weeks of celebration.

In Wicca, and modern Paganism, the Winter Solstice is the time of new beginnings, a time to reflect on the past and project for the future. Magickally, the Winter Solstice affords us a perfect time to formulate a plan of action, a goal we can work towards during the coming year. (See Appendix A for the Yule Ritual.)

Magickal Activities
The Yule Candle

Traditionally, the Yule Candle was a very large ornamental candle, usually blue, green, or red in color. The candle should be large enough to last the entire Yule (Christmas) season. The candle should only be lit and extinguished by the head of the household. It is best placed on the mantle over the hearth or on the sill of the window in the front of the house. The candle must be extinguished with a candle-snuffer or pair of tongs; to blow it out will bring bad luck. Each night, all the members of the household gather as a family prayer is read and the candle is lit. Before retiring for the night, the prayer is again read and the candle extinguished.

Sample Prayer

Let hope and peace come with this light,
To illuminate and cheer the way.
For from the darkness of the night,
Will come a better—brighter day.

Solstice Wishing Balls

This is a fun activity for the whole family, or it can be used to enhance the Winter Solstice religious rites. Participants write out their wishes on small pieces of paper. They will then be placed inside of a hollow Christmas tree ornament. The ornament is then filled with allspice for wealth, rosemary for protection, cinnamon for success, and coriander for health. The loop at the top is secured with gold, blue, red, and green ribbons. The ornaments can then be blessed during ritual and later hung over the main doorway of the household.

22 December

Hanukkah

Hanukkah is an eight-day Jewish festival. Its date is calculated from the 25th day of Kislev, the third month of the lunar year, which places it near the Winter Solstice. According to the *Apocrypha*, the Syrian king Epiphanes (Antiochus IV) in

162 B.C. profaned the temple at Jerusalem by having an altar placed in it for the Greek God Zeus. This provoked a rebellion led by Judah Maccabee, and the temple was then cleansed and a new altar was then constructed and dedicated in 165 B.C. Legend has that there was only a limited amount of oil for relighting the perpetual lamp that adorned the altar. Miraculously the lamp burned for eight days. Thus Hanukkah, the Festival of Lights, was born. Traditionally, a *menorah* or candelabra is lit, one candle on the first night and then one each night thereafter for eight consecutive nights. Hanukkah is a time of joy and celebration. Games are played, gifts are exchanged, and elaborate feasts are held that usually include latkes or potato pancakes.

Potato Latkes

4 large potatoes, peeled and grated
2 eggs
1 tsp. salt
¼ tsp. baking powder
¼ onion, chopped
¼ cup flour
¼ tsp. pepper
Oil for frying

Place the potatoes, onion, and eggs in a large bowl; add flour, salt, pepper, and baking powder and mix well. Heat about ½ cup oil in skillet. Drop mixture by spoonfuls into the hot oil. Cook until golden brown, about three minutes on each side. Drain on paper towels. Makes about 24 small pancakes. The latkes are best served hot with applesauce.

23 December
Larentalia

The ancient Roman festival of Larnetalia, held on December 23, consisted of funeral rites held at the tomb of the Goddess *Acca Larentia*. The rites were conducted by the pontiffs and the *Flamen Quirnalis.*

Acca Larnetia, or Larentia, was an obscure Roman Goddess that appears to have been connected to the founding of Rome. In one of her legends she is the wife of Faustulus, the heardsman who found Romulus and Remus with the wolf—the legendary founders of Rome.

24 and 25 December
Christmas Eve, Christmas, Yule

It is generally accepted that the birth of Christ on December 24th is the invention of some overzealous authors who were trying to create some sort of symmetry between Paganism and Christianity. According to the late fourth-century *Scriptor Syrus*, it was the custom of the Pagans to celebrate the birthday of the sun on December 25, at which time they kindled lights in token of festivity. The Christians also participated in these solemnities and revelries. Accordingly, when the administrants of the church observed that the Christians had a preference for the festival, they took counsel and resolved that the true Nativity should be solemnized on that day.

The Pagan feast that was replaced by Christmas was of far older origins and may have been built upon the cult of Mithras, who, for the Persians, was the creator of the universe and manifestation of the Creative Logos, or Word. His birth on December 25 was witnessed by shepherds. After many deeds, he held a last supper with his disciples and then returned to heaven. Some believe that, had Christianity not taken hold when it did, Mithraism very well might have become the world religion.

For more that three centuries *Christ Mass* was a moveable feast, celebrated on the Epiphany (January 6), the day that, according to biblical account, Jesus manifested himself to the Magi. The Western date of December 25 was fixed to coincide with the Roman midwinter festival of the Kalends, which was preceded by seven days of tribute to their God of agriculture, Saturn.

Many of the Yuletide customs we observe today were common to various thanksgiving days and new year's rites. For example, the hanging of greenery comes from an old ivy-worshiping cult dating back to the Dionysian revels in ancient Greece; mistletoe was valued—almost worshiped—by the Druids; and gift exchange most likely generated with the Saturnalia.

MERRY CHRISTMAS

The Christmas tree was introduced by the Prince Albert of Saxony in 1844 and was an adaption of the *Paradeisbaum* (decorated tree of life) from the medieval drama of the *Tannenbaum*.

26 December–1 January
Kwanzaa

Kwanzaa, Swahili for "First Fruits," is the traditional African festival that has been embraced by many African Americans as an alternative to Christmas. It is regarded as a time of thanksgiving and celebrates the first harvest of their crops with feasting and dancing.

As an American holiday, *Kwanzaa* was adopted in 1966 and extends African Americans the opportunity to renew their ties with family and their African heritage. Candles are lit each day of the festival, and stories of the African way of life are told. On the last day of the festival, games are played, elders honored, and presents exchanged between the children. Some of the traditional symbols of Kwanzaa are:

Mkeke: A straw hat that represents foundation.

Mahinde: A corn plant, the symbol of growth.

Kinara: The seven-pronged candle
           holder.

Matunda: First fruits of the harvest.

Kikombe: A goblet or cup used to toast
           the ancestors.

Zawadi: Gifts of love.

27 December
St John's Day

St. John, the son of Zebedee and the brother of St. James the Great, was an apostle of the Lord Jesus Christ in the first year of his ministry. He became the "beloved disciple" and the only one of the 12 who did not betray the Savior in the hour of His Passion. John stood faithfully at the Cross, and the Savior thus made St. John the guardian of his mother, the Virgin Mary. He lived to an extremely old age and died at Ephesus about the year 100. St. John is the patron of booksellers, publishers, and writers.

28 and 29 December
Holy Innocents' Day, Feast of Fools

Holy Innocents' Day is the third day of Christmas and considered to be the unluckiest days of the year. It is held that on this day all children under 2 years of age were slaughtered by Herod in an attempt to eliminate the Infant Jesus—the predicted king of the Jews. The star is associated with this day, and the Innocents are the patrons of all children and foundlings.

A popular holiday during the Middle Ages, the "Feast of Fools" captured the light-hearted spirit of the Saturnalia. On this day, roles were reversed, masters waited on their servants, and the often-puritanical reverence of the Christmas season was replaced with frivolity and pleasure.

30 and 31 December
Mumming, New Year's Eve, Hogmany

The end of December ushers in the new year, a time of anticipation and celebration. For our pre-Christian ancestors, most of the New Year's festivities were designed to ward off the barrenness of Winter and insure the fertility of Spring. This was accomplished with the actual or symbolic killing of the king of the old year and the welcoming of a new king—a metaphor still dramatized in the popular British mumming play.

It was during the 19th century, when the hustle of the Christmas Day celebrations were over and the new year was fast approaching, that the mummers took to the streets, pubs, and private homes to act out their plays. Masked and costumed, they portrayed three different themes: the Hero-Combat of St. George, the "Sword Dance," and the Plough or Wooing play. Of the three, the Hero-Combat was the most favored.

The central part of the play begins with the Hero fighting an opposing champion or, occasionally, a whole succession of enemies—the Black Prince, the Turkish Knight, or the Bold Slasher. After a spirited battle, in most but not all cases, the villain is slain. Suddenly a doctor appears, who boasts lengthily (with a great deal of buffoonery) of his skill and travels, after which the dead man suddenly regenerates. Once the mummers have been paid, they journey to their next performance.

It might not be as well known as Christmas or New Year's Eve, but *Hogmanay* is still celebrated in parts of England and Scotland. Although the word *Hogmanay* has never been satisfactorily established, it very well may come from the Anglo-Saxon *Haleg Monath* (Holy Month) or from the giant Gogmagog or Hogmagog, guardians of the cities of London and Plymouth. For the most part, Hogmanay is met with massive enthusiasm. Parties are held, people ring bells, fireworks are set off, and everyone makes a conscious effort to make a clean break with the past by making New Year's resolutions.

Scotland has always made more of Hogmanay than England and still has a variety of customs associated with the holiday. Some of these include divination, of which Bibliomancy is the most popular. The Family Bible is prayed over, and then the person seeking his or her future will open the Bible at random. Without looking, a verse is marked with the index finger and then read. Whatever the verse discusses will be the person's fortune for the year. Another popular custom is to open the back door of the home and then close it just before midnight to let out all of the bad luck. At the stroke of midnight, the front door is then opened to let in the good luck. Finally, Hogmanay is a favored time for predicting the weather by observing the direction of the wind with this old Scots rhyme:

> *If New Year's Eve night-wind blow south,*
> *That betokens warmth and growth.*
> *If west, much milk, and fish in the sea,*
> *If north, much cold and storms will be.*
> *If east, the trees will bear much fruit,*
> *If north-east, flee it, man and brute.*

Magickal Activity
Balloon Magick

You will need a helium-filled balloon for each participant, string, and a small square of paper. Each balloon chosen should be a color that reflects the individual's desire (see the following chart).

Red:	Courage, strength, and power.	Blue:	Creativity and peace.
Green:	Money, luck, and personal goals.	Black:	Protection and release.
Pink:	Friendship and love.	Yellow:	Selling and communication.
Orange:	Action and attraction.	White:	Spiritual and psychic awareness.

Ten minutes before the hour of midnight, each person writes a wish on a small square of paper. Using the string, attach the paper to the balloon. At the stroke of midnight, each participant chants the following and then releases a balloon:

> *Float now free,*
> *Bring to me,*
> *What I wish*
> *So mote it be!*

Once the balloon has been released, it is best not to dwell on the wish but to let it go so that it will manifest.

The New Year has always been looked to with great anticipation and celebration. In the past, New Year's festivities were supposed to ward off the barrenness of Winter and insure the fertility of Spring.

Happy New Year!

Appendix A
Seasonal Sabbat Celebrations

The Sabbats occur approximately every six weeks, beginning with Yule on December 21. For those who practice Wicca, these Sabbats are more than just a change of season and weather; they are a reflection of the cyclic processes of life, death, and rebirth. Frequently, they trigger a response deep within the mind of the believer that leaves a lasting spiritual impression. From a mystical perspective, they provide the practitioner with a time to reconnect with Nature and the forces that maintain the momentum of the universe, the God, and the Goddess.

The eight Sabbat celebrations presented here are complete and can be used as they appear. However, there is no reason they cannot be altered or used as outlines for your own creativity. If you have special customs or family traditions that you are especially fond of, feel free to include them where and when they seem appropriate.

Yule
Ritual Tools, Symbols, and Decorations

Altar Decorations: Red altar cloth; red or green altar candles; sprigs of holly tied with red and green ribbons; bayberry candle; poinsettia plant; wand tied with red and green ribbon; chalice covered with a gold cloth; red and white wine; ritual cakes.

Symbols: Yule log; mistletoe tied with green ribbon; Yule tree decorated with colorful ornaments and lights; gifts wrapped in bright seasonal paper; bowl filled with fresh fruits and nuts; wand tied with red and green ribbon; talismans to represents personal desires and goals.

The Ceremony

Light the right altar candle and then the left one as you say the following:

Right   *Blessed be the fire of faith, which brings forth the light.*

Left   *Blessed be the light of the world, which brings forth life.*

Cast the circle and call in the Guardians. Face the altar, anoint the forehead with seasonal oil, and speak the following blessing:

> *Blessed be the White Goddess,*
> *Blessed be the Sacrificed King.*
> *Blessed be the Spiritual Seed,*
> *Blessed be the newborn Sun.*

Say the following blessing, and light the bayberry candle:

> *Lord and Lady of the night,*
>   *Of mist and of moonlight.*
> *Though you are seldom seen,*
>   *I meet you in heart, mind, and dream.*
> *Bless my thoughts, works, and deeds,*
>   *That they shall fulfill my wishes and needs.*
> *On this night I honor thee,*
>   *To make my desire a reality.*
> *My love I now give to thee,*
>   *For your blessings, So mote it be!*

Offer the candle at each of the four quadrants as you speak the following accordingly:

East   *Blessed be the light, coming from the East that brings insight and wisdom.*

South   *Blessed be the fire, coming from the South that brings strength and power.*

West   *Blessed be the moisture, coming from the West that brings control and dominion.*

North   *Blessed the fertile earth of the North that provides
         manifestation of desire.*

Place the candle back on the altar. Take a few moments to meditate on the meaning of the ritual. Relax, invoke the God, and then invoke the Goddess. At this point, you will want to energize the bayberry candle with your thoughts and desires. Place your hands over the candle, express your desire, and then chant the following:

> *God of Glory, God of Light,*
> *Bless me on this Solstice night.*

Pause and then bless the wine and bread through the *Rite of Union* and *Blessing of the Bread* ceremonies. Begin your closing segment of the rite by offering this blessing:

> *Within my heart is devoted feeling,*
> > *Vainly should my lips express.*
> *I come before your altar kneeling,*
> > *And pray this time and place you bless.*

Dismiss the Guardians and extinguish the altar candles beginning with the left:

Left   *Blessed be the faith that brought forth light.*
Right   *Blessed be the light that brought forth life.*

Take up the circle, and allow the bayberry candle to burn out.

Imbolg: Brigantia
Ritual Tools, Symbols, and Decorations

Altar Decorations: White, silver, or pink altar cloth; white altar candles; bouquet of pink rose buds tied with silver ribbon; rose-colored candle; wand tied with pink and silver ribbon; chalice covered with a silver or white cloth; white wine; ritual cakes.

Symbols: Brighid's Cross; crown of candles; candles engraved with pink or silver hearts; heart-shaped boxes decorated with pink roses to place wishes in; white lace potpourri pouches filled with violet, rose, and heather and tied with pink ribbon; clear quartz crystals.

The Ceremony

Light the right altar candle and then the left one as you say the following:

Right   *Fearless Lord, Protector, and Father of All,*
            Bring forth light, life, and wisdom.

Left   *White Maiden, Gentle Mother, Silent One,*
            Deliver us from ignorance and darkness.

Cast the circle, and call in the Guardians. Face the altar, anoint the forehead with seasonal oil, and speak the following blessing:

> *My Lady who has been with me from the beginning*
> *You are my light and life.*
> *My Lord who comes from the glory of the Lady,*
> *You are my strength and power.*
> *Let now the dawn and spring of life come forth.*
> *Let now the fire and spirit of life come forth.*
> *Let now the passion and love of life come forth.*
> *Let now the balance and wisdom of life come forth.*

Light the rose-colored candle as you speak the following:

> *I pray, banish the Winter and bring back the Spring,*
>   *Let the light and life come to every living thing.*
> *The glory of the God and Goddess I now behold,*
>   *For all that is given shall return threefold.*
> *As I revel in the warmth of this Divine light,*
>   *I pray, bless and protect me form this night.*

Pick up the bouquet of flowers and hold it in offering as you say:

> *Lady of Light, Wise One, thou art pure in spirit,*
> *And love eternal.*
> *Lord of Fire, Passionate One thou art true force,*
> *And endless power.*

Place the bouquet on the altar in front of the candle. Take a few moments to meditate on the meaning of the ritual. Relax. Invoke the God and then the Goddess. At this point you will want to energize the rose-colored candle with your thoughts and desires. Place your hands over the candle, express your desire, and then chant the following:

> *Passion and fire,*
> *Bring forth desire.*

Pause and then bless the wine and bread through the *Rite of Union* and *Blessing of the Bread* ceremonies. Begin your closing segment of the rite by offering this blessing:

> *Within my heart is devoted feeling,*
> > *Vainly should my lips express.*
> *I come before your altar kneeling,*
> > *And pray this time and place you bless.*

Dismiss the Guardians and extinguish the altar candles, beginning with the left:

Left   *Lady of Light, Wise One, thou art pure spirit*
         And love eternal.

Right   *Lord of Fire, Passionate One, thou art true force*
         And endless power.

Take up the circle, and allow the rose-colored candle to burn out. Dry the pink rose buds in the bouquet and use in incense.

Ostara, The Spring Equinox
Ritual Tools, Symbols, and Decorations

Altar Decorations: Lilac or pastel blue altar cloth; lilac or pastel blue altar candles; lilies tied with lilac ribbon; lilac-scented pillar candle; wand tied with lilac or pale blue ribbon; chalice covered with a lilac or pale blue cloth; rose wine; egg-shaped container filled with seeds for blessing.

Symbols: Decorated egg; baskets filled with eggs; egg-shaped boxes; rabbits; bouquets of lilies tied with lilac and white ribbon; wild-flower chain necklaces; seeds and packages of seeds tied together with yellow and light green ribbon.

The Ceremony

Light the right altar candle and then the left one as you say the following:

Right   *Lord of the sky now descend,*
         Move the spirit of my soul.
         Renew within the vital force,
         Give me energy, make me whole.

Left   *Lady from the earth now come,*
         Lead me into the new dawning day.

> *Protect me from the passions of man,*
> *Guide me along thy secret way.*

Cast the circle, and call in the Guardians. Face the altar, anoint the forehead with seasonal oil, and light the lilac-scented pillar candle as you speak the following blessing:

> *By the power of air, fire, water, and earth,*
> *To Spring and joy, oh Goddess give birth.*

Pick up the lilac-scented candle and proceed to offer it at each of the quadrants. Begin in the East by saying:

East   *Element of air, power of the mind,*
              Your intellect and wisdom I now bind.

South   *Element of fire, power of the soul,*
              Your strength and fortitude make me whole.

West   *Element of water, power of the heart,*
              Your beauty and grace, now impart.

North   *Element of earth, power of the will,*
              Your force and focus within me still.

Place the candle in the center of the altar. Pick up the egg and ask the following blessing:

> *White Maiden, Enchantress, Goddess of fire,*
>   *Mother of hearth, home, and desire.*
> *You form the passion within the great God's heart,*
>   *So that within you the seed of life he does impart.*
> *O Great Lady, you are the Queen of Spring,*
>   *As you bring light and life to every living thing.*

Place the egg, filled with the seeds, on the altar in front of the candle. Take a few moments to meditate on the meaning of the ritual. Relax. Invoke the Goddess and then the God. At this point, you will want to energize the lilac candle with your thoughts and desires. Place your hands over the candle, express your desire, and then chant the following:

> *Blessed be the flower and seed,*
>   *That will grant to me what I need.*

Pause, and bless the wine and bread through the *Rite of Union* and *Blessing of the Bread* ceremonies. Begin your closing segment of the rite by offering this blessing:

> *Within my heart is devoted feeling,*
> *Vainly should my lips express.*
> *I come before your altar kneeling,*
> *And pray this time and place you bless.*

Pick up the candle and proceed to offer it at each of the quadrants in closing. Begin in the North by saying:

North   *May the spirit of earth bring me wisdom.*

West   *May the spirit of water bring me control.*

South   *May the spirit of fire bring me inspiration.*

East   *May the spirit of air bring me awareness.*

Dismiss the Guardians and extinguish the altar candles, beginning with the left one:

Left   *Lady, Enchantress, Mother of the earth,*
         To my dreams and wishes give birth.

Right   *Lord, Father of light, glowing sun.*
         Let my will and work be done.

Take up the circle, and allow the lilac-scented candle to burn out. When the weather permits, take the seeds out of the plastic egg and plant them. Save the egg to use again next year.

Beltane
Ritual Tools, Symbols, and Decorations
Altar Decorations: Green altar cloth; green altar candles; vases filled with fresh flowers; small crown of fresh flowers; green pillar candle; wand tied with seven different-colored ribbons; chalice covered with green cloth; May wine ritual cakes.

Symbols: May pole; wand; crown of flowers; candles tied with seven different-colored ribbons; baskets of fresh flowers tied with colored ribbon; branches of rowan tied with green ribbon; green candle in a cauldron; bonfires.

The Ceremony

Light the right altar candle and then the left one as you say the following:

Right   *Blessed be the Lord of light and power,*
           He transforms my soul from this hour.

Left   *Blessed Be the Lady of love and passion,*
           My heart and future She shall fashion.

Cast the circle and call in the Guardians. Face the altar, anoint the forehead with seasonal oil, and speak the following blessing:

> *I pray, Glorious Goddess of the moon,*
> > *As I stand between day and night.*
> *Your heavenly presences grant me a soon,*
> > *As darkness gives way to light.*

Light the green pillar candle. Pick up the candle and hold it in offering as you speak the following:

> *Thou who rises from the raging sea,*
> > *Shall now accept thy destiny.*
> *Now, Great Lady of the inner earth,*
> > *To the land of promise come and give birth.*
> *So that all the seed, fruit, and grain,*
> > *Shall in abundance come forth again.*

Pick up the crown of flowers, hold it in offering as you invoke the Goddess, and then place the crown of flowers on your head. Pick up the wand and invoke the God. Still holding the wand, proceed to each quadrant and ask for blessing. Begin in the East by saying:

East   *I ask for guidance form the realm of the Eternal Spirit,*
           Bless me with inspiration and insight.

South   *I ask for guidance from the realm of the Divine Spark,*
           Bless me with energy and power.

West   *I ask for guidance form the realm of the Final Atonement,*
           Bless me with wisdom and control.

North   *I ask for guidance from the realm of the Ultimate Creation,*
           Bless me with skill and ability.

Place the crown of flowers on the altar. Set the green pillar candle inside of the crown, and place the wand in front of them. Place your hands over the candle and express your desire. Then chant the following:

> *Lovely Lady of the moon,*
> *Grant my needs and wishes soon.*

Pause, and bless the wine and bread through the *Rite of Union* and *Blessing of the Bread* ceremonies. Begin your closing segment of the rite by offering this blessing:

> *Within my heart is devoted feeling,*
> *Vainly should my lips express.*
> *I come before your altar kneeling,*
> *And pray this time and place you bless.*

Dismiss the Guardians and extinguish the altar candles, beginning with the left:

Left   *Blessed shall be this time of enlightenment,*
       My seeds have been sown and my labors shall be rewarded.

Right   *Blessed shall be the rewards of the spirit,*
       May I always remember to give as I have received.

Take up the circle, and allow the green pillar candle to burn out. When the candle has burned out, take the crown of flowers to a river or stream. Toss the crown into the water, asking the Goddess to bless your goals and help you manifest your desire.

Midsummer, The Summer Solstice
Ritual Tools, Symbols, and Decorations

Altar Decorations: Bright yellow altar cloth; sunshine yellow altar candles; bouquet of marigolds tied with yellow and green ribbon; wand tied with yellow ribbon; floating candle in a bowl of water; chalice covered with a yellow cloth; red and white wine; sun-shaped ritual cakes.

Symbols: Wheel tied with colored ribbon; floating candles in bowls of colored water; wands made of oak or hawthorn; birds and horned animals; the chariot; sun talismans made of gold; bonfire; wishing wells and fountains.

The Ceremony

Light the right altar candle and then the left one as you say the following:

Right   *Lord of the sun, God of truth and might,*
          In your honor, do I this candle light.

Left   *Lady of the moon, Goddess of celestial power,*
          I beseech thee to bless me from this hour.

Cast the circle and call in the Guardians. Face the altar, and light the floating candle. Pick up the bowl with the candle in it and proceed to the Eastern Quadrant. Address the Eastern Quadrant as you hold the bowl in offering, and then proceed to the next Quadrant. Each time, hold the bowl in offering as you say the appropriate line:

East   *Let now the winds of consciousness bring forth insight and wisdom.*

South   *Let now the fires of awareness bring forth motivation and inspiration.*

West   *Let now the waves of completeness bring forth love and understanding.*

North   *Let now the blossoming fertile earth bring forth the manifestation of desire.*

Place the bowl back on the altar. Turn, face the Southern Quadrant, and say:

> *To the Great Lord of the sun,*
>   *My gratitude I do show.*
> *As in life and spirit,*
>   *I work to progress and grow.*
> *I thank you Father of light,*
>   *By each and every work and deed.*
> *That all I have and shall receive,*
>   *Is all that I shall ever want or need.*

Now, turn and face the altar invoke the God and then the Goddess. Take a moment to meditate on the meaning of the ritual and season. At this point, you will want to energize the floating candle with your own wishes. Place your hands over the candle, express your desire, and then chant the following:

> *Sun and flame,*
> *Bring joy and gain.*

Pause, and bless the wine and bread through the *Rite of Union* and *Blessing of the Bread* ceremony. Begin your closing segment of the rite by offering this blessing:

> *Within my heart is devoted feeling,*
> *Vainly should my lips express.*
> *I come before your altar kneeling,*
> *And pray this time and place you bless.*

Dismiss the Guardians and extinguish the altar candles, beginning with the left:

Left   *Lady of the moon, Goddess of celestial power,*
             I bid thee bless and protect me from this hour.

Right   *Lord of the sun, God of truth and might,*
             Guide and guard me as I go into the night.

Take up the circle, and allow the floating candle to burn out.

Lughnasa
Ritual Tools, Symbols, and Decorations

Altar Decorations: Gold or yellow altar cloth; gold altar candles; four ears of corn, each tied with a yellow and orange ribbon; small basket of fruit; gold-colored pillar candle; chalice covered with a yellow cloth; red and white wine; cornbread or ritual cakes.

Symbols: Corn; bread and all baked goods; the pentacle; the hearth, broom, and things connected with the home; baskets filled with corn and fresh vegetables; gift baskets filled with fresh baked goods and tied with gold ribbons; dried corn husks for making corn dollies.

The Ceremony

Light the right candle and then the left as you say the following:

Right   *My Lord is the passion,*
             He brings forth the light,
             The harvest is of his seed.

Left   *My Lady is the power,*
             She brings forth the life,
             The harvest is her reward.

Cast the circle and call in the Guardians. Face the altar, and speak the following blessing:

> *My Lady, I know that naught receives naught,*
> *That I shall reap, that which I have sowed.*
> *On this night, shall I receive accordingly,*
> *For nothing is withheld from those deserving.*
> *Blessed shall be the Goddess,*
> *And blessed shall be the fruits of my labor.*

Pick up the four ears of corn. Hold them in offering and ask the following blessing on them:

> *Corn and grain are of this earth,*
> > *With love and work I gave them birth.*
> *Though they were just once small seeds,*
> > *Through them I achieved my wishes and needs.*

Proceed to offer, and then place the corn at each of the four quadrants. Walk to the East chanting as you go:

> *As the corn, I am reborn.*

Offer the corn to the East. Place it next to the Eastern Quadrant candle. Then proceed to the South. Do the same for the West and the North. Then return to the altar.

Say the following blessing, and light the gold pillar candle:

> *My Lord and Lady you shall provide,*
> > *Long after all has withered and died.*
> *Though you have given me life through the land,*
> > *What I know hold is the work of my hand.*
> *I shall always remember, just as the corn,*
> > *That I am ever living, dying, and reborn.*
>
> *As the corn, I am reborn!*

Place the candle in the center of the altar on the pentacle, and invoke the God, and then the Goddess. Take a moment to meditate on the meaning of the ritual and season. At this point, you will want to energize the candle with your own wishes. Place your hands over the candle, express your desire, and then chant the following:

> *Corn and grain*
> *Bring joy and gain!*

Pause, and bless the wine and bread through the *Rite of Union,* and *Blessing of the Bread* ceremonies. Begin your closing segment of the rite by offering this blessing:

> *Within my heart is devoted feeling,*
> > *Vainly should my lips express.*
> *I come before your altar kneeling,*
> > *And pray this time and place you bless.*

Dismiss the Guardians and extinguish the altar candles, beginning with the left:

Left   *Blessed be the Maiden, Mother, and Crone*
        Bring me blessings from your harvest home.

Right   *Blessed be the King of corn and grain,*
        As now the season of abundance begins to wane.

Take up the circle and allow the gold candle to burn out. Hang the ears of corn to dry. When the ears of corn have completely dried, save them to make your corn-baba for Autumn Equinox.

Mabon, Autumn Equinox
Ritual Tools, Symbols, and Decorations

Decorations: Orange, red, or brown altar cloth; orange or red altar candles; corn-baba cornucopia filled with fruit and vegetables; red apple-shaped candle; wand tied with orange, red, and brown ribbon; apple-flavored wine or hard cider; ritual cakes.

Symbols: Corn-baba; apples; scarecrow; cornucopia; sickle; dried gourds; broom; cauldron; apple dolls; baskets tied with orange, red, and brown ribbon; dried flowers; leaves; bonfires.

The Ceremony

Light the right altar candle and then the left one as you say the following:

Right   *Lord of the sun,*
        Pulsing bright.
        Cast away the shadows,
        Bring forth the light.

Left   *Lady of the moon,*
        Jewel of power.
        Bless this sacred space,
        From this hour.

Cast the circle, and call in the Guardians. Face the altar, anoint the forehead with seasonal oil, and speak the following blessing:

> *Blessed Be the Lady.*
> *Blessed Be the Lord.*
> *Blessed Be the corn.*
> *Blessed Be the harvest.*

Say the following blessing, and light the apple candle:

> *Lord of corn, barley, and rye,*
> > *Golden Sun, ruler of the sky.*
> *Lady of milk, honey, and wine*
> > *Silver moon, Mistress most Divine.*
> *Fruit of field, passion and fire,*
> > *Light the way, fulfill desire.*
> *Blessed Be the Lord and Lady!*

Place the candle back on the altar and pick up the corn-baba. Hold the corn-baba in offering as you ask this blessing:

> *Golden-haired mother,*
> > *Red dying king.*
> *Leaves are falling,*
> > *And sickles gleam.*
> *Hearty is the harvest,*
> > *Blessed is the corn.*
> *What withers and dies,*
> > *Always is reborn.*

Still holding the corn-baba, proceed to offer it at each of the quadrants. Begin in the East by saying:

East   *Element of air, power of the mind,*
        Your intellect and wisdom I now bind.

South   *Element of fire, power of the soul,*
        Your strength and fortitude make me whole.

West   *Element of water, power of the heart,*
        Your beauty and grace now impart.

North   *Element of earth, power of the will,*
        Your force and focus within me still.

Place the corn-baba in the center of the altar, and invoke the God and then the Goddess. Take a moment to meditate on the meaning of the ritual and season. At this point, you will want to energize the corn-baba with your own wishes. Place your hands over the corn-baba, express your desire, and then chant the following:

> *Blessed be the harvest,*
> > *Blessed be the home.*
> *Blessed be the grain*
> > *And all that I have sown.*

Pause, and bless the wine or cider and bread through the *Rite of Union,* and *Blessing of the Bread* ceremonies. Begin your closing segment of the rite by offering this blessing:

> *Within my heart is devoted feeling,*
> > *Vainly should my lips express.*
> *I come before your altar kneeling,*
> > *And pray this time and place you bless.*

Pick up the corn-baba and proceed to offer it in closing at each of the quadrants. Begin in the North by saying:

North   *May the spirit of earth bring me wisdom.*

West   *May the spirit of water bring me control.*

South   *May the spirit of fire bring me inspiration.*

East   *May the spirit of air bring me awareness.*

Dismiss the Guardians and extinguish the altar candles, beginning with the left one:

Left   *Lady of the Silver Moon,*
        Mistress of this holy earth.
        Grant to me a special boon,
        To my wishes and needs give birth.

Right   *Lord of the Golden Sun,*
        Master of the forest and field.

> *Let your will and work be done,*
> *Protect me with your sword and shield.*

Take up the circle and allow the apple candle to burn out. Hang the corn-baba over the main entrance to your home. If you own your own business and want to increase sales or product value, place the corn-baba next to the cash register.

Samhain
Ritual Tools, Symbols, and Decorations

Altar Decorations: Black altar cloth; red altar candles; cauldron or pot with water and a floating candle; black pillar candle; bowl of apples; wand tied with black ribbon; lighted pumpkins; black silk pouch; chalice covered with a black cloth; red and white wine.

Symbols: Jack-o-lanterns; cauldron; scrying mirror or bowl; tarot cards; torches; bonfires; graveyard; tombstone; broom; cornstalks; runes for casting; photographs of departed ancestors; oak and hazel wands tied with black ribbon.

The Ceremony

Light the right altar candle and then the left one as you say the following:

Right   *Blessed Be the Dying King,*
            And the sacrifice of blood He shed.
            For He alone shall guide me,
            Through the time of dark and dread.

Left   *Blessed Be the Death Crone,*
            And Her silent tides of death and birth.
            For She alone brings love,
            Life and wisdom to this earth.

At this point, you will light each of the tea lights inside of the four pumpkins. Pick up a pumpkin and place it in the East as you acknowledge the Quadrant. Then place one in the South, West, and North, each time acknowledging the Quadrant:

East   *Let there be light in the East, the home of the Eternal Spirit.*
South   *Let there be light in the South, the home of the Divine Spark*
West   *Let there be light in the West, the home of rest and regeneration.*

North   *Let there be light in the North, the home of the final atonement.*

Cast the circle and call in the Guardians. Face the altar, anoint the forehead with seasonal oil, and then speak the following:

Death brings life, life brings death.

Light the black pillar candle and say the following blessing:

Let this flame radiate through the night,
Bring forth great wisdom and much insight.
At this sacred time, and in this holy place,
I beckon those of the past to come and share my space.

Pick up the bowl of apples. Hold the bowl in offering and ask the following blessing:

The land has died, the earth is cold,
*   The Horned One comes from times of old.*
He brings the word, He is the death,
*   He whispers my name with icy breath.*
Come close ancestral spirits of Hallows' night,
*   Gather around my cauldron light.*
For all across the land, death does roam,
*   But here the Lord protects his own.*

Place the apples around the cauldron. Light the candle inside the cauldron, and invoke the God and then the Goddess. After the invocations, take time to do some divination or meditation on the meaning of the ritual. Next, you will want to energize the protection bag you made. Place your hands over the bag, express your desire, and then chant the following:

Blithe spirits blessing, from cauldron light,
Protect me now, with all your might.

Pause, and bless the wine or cider and bread through the *Rite of Union,* and *Blessing of the Bread* ceremonies. Begin your closing segment of the rite by offering this blessing:

Within my heart is devoted feeling,
*   Vainly should my lips express.*
I come before your altar kneeling,
*   And pray this time and place you bless.*

Beginning in the North, extinguish the candles in the pumpkins as follows:

North   *Death now brings darkness to the North, the home of the final atonement.*

West   *Death now brings darkness to the West, the home of rest and regeneration.*

South   *Death now brings darkness to the South, the home of the Divine Spark.*

East   *Death now brings darkness to the East, the home of the Eternal Spirit.*

Dismiss the Guardians and extinguish the altar candles, beginning with the left:

Left   *Blessed be Death Crone,*
       Transform my soul this night.

Right   *Blessed be Lord of Death,*
       Bring me rest and quiet.

Take up the circle and allow the floating candle and the black pillar candle to burn out. Place the protection where you feel it will do the most good—in your car, in your desk at work, or in a special place in your home.

Appendix B
Correspondences and Charts

Elemental Correspondences

Air

Direction:	East
Archangel:	Raphael
Qualities:	Light, intellect, new beginnings
Color:	Blue
Meaning:	To know
Zodiac:	Gemini, Aquarius, Libra
Tattvic symbol:	Circle
Season:	Spring
Magickal Tool:	Wand or dagger
Animal:	Eagle
Symbols:	Sky, wind, clouds, incense
Elemental Spirit:	Sylphs
Elemental King:	Paralda
Positive Characteristics:	Intelligence, mind, psychic abilities
Negative Characteristics:	Lack of communication, gossip, memory problems

Fire

Direction:	South
Archangel:	Michael
Qualities:	Activity, force, willpower
Color:	Red
Meaning:	To will
Zodiac:	Aries, Leo, Sagittarius
Tattvic Symbol:	Triangle
Season:	Summer
Magickal Tool:	Dagger or wand
Animal:	Lion
Symbols:	Fire, sun, passion and candles
Elemental Spirit:	Salamanders
Elemental King:	Djyn
Positive Characteristics:	Energy, enthusiasm, will, strength
Negative Characteristics:	Greed, vengeance, ego, jealousy

Water

Direction:	West
Archangel:	Gabriel
Qualities:	Heavy, passive, receptivity
Color:	Green
Meaning:	To dare
Zodiac:	Cancer, Scorpio, Pisces
Tattvic Symbol:	Crescent Moon
Season:	Fall
Magickal Tool:	Chalice
Animal:	Snake, scorpion
Symbols:	Waves, bodies of water, cups
Elemental Spirit:	Undines
Elemental King:	Niksa
Positive Characteristics:	Sensitivity, compassion, grace
Negative Characteristics:	Overly emotional, insecurities, lack of self-esteem

Earth

Direction:	North
Archangel:	Auriel (Uriel)
Qualities:	Stability, growth, manifestation
Color:	Yellow
Meaning:	To keep silent
Zodiac:	Taurus, Virgo, Capricorn
Tattvic Symbol:	Square
Season:	Winter
Magickal Tool:	Pentacle
Animal:	Bull
Symbols:	Mountains, forest, stone, salt
Elemental Spirit:	Gnomes and trolls.
Elemental King:	Gob
Positive Characteristics:	Endurance, reliability, material world
Negative Characteristics:	Materialistic, non-progressive, lazy

Herbs of The Zodiac

ARIES (The Ram) fire, cardinal:	Allspice, cactus, dragon's blood, pepper
TAURUS (The Bull) earth, fixed:	Alfalfa, honeysuckle, primrose, tulip
GEMINI (The Twins) air, mutable:	Almond, clover, lavender, pine
CANCER (The Crab) water, cardinal:	Lemon balm, cucumber, lilac, thyme
LEO (The Lion) fire, fixed:	Basil, coriander, hyssop, tobacco
VIRGO (The Virgin) earth, mutable:	Corn, magnolia, vetivert, wheat
LIBRA (The Scales) air, cardinal:	Broom, eyebright, lily of the valley, mint
SCORPIO (The Scorpion) water, fixed:	Belladonna, hemlock, lotus, willow
SAGITTARIUS (The Archer) fire, mutable:	Asafoetida, garlic, rosemary, wormwood

Capricorn (The Goat) earth, cardinal:
Cypress, patchouli, mugwort, vervain

Aquarius (The Water Bearer) air, fixed:
Benzoin, linden, mistletoe, papyrus

Pisces (The Fishes) water, mutable: Crocus, heather, myrrh, yarrow

Corespondences for the Days of the Week

Sunday corresponds to the sun and the first day of the week. It represents high masculine energy and is a very good time for individual, positive, creative works. Sunday is a good time to begin spells that are aimed at acquiring money, health, friendship, and patronage for business.

Monday, the second day of the week, aligns with the moon. This is a day of high feminine energy and a good time to develop self-expression, seek inspiration, and work to enhance psychic abilities. Monday is a good time to begin spells that deal with initiating changes and personal growth of the feminine aspect.

Tuesday belongs to Mars, the god of war. This is a time of dynamic energy and pure raw power. Tuesday is a good time to begin spells that will overcome rivalry or malice, develop physical strength and courage, or help protect one's property and investments. It is also a good time for military matters and anything that requires a lot of force, power, and energy to activate.

Wednesday is associated with Mercury and the ability to communicate. The power of Mercury is what helps you get your ideas out there. Wednesday is a good time to do spells where communication is involved, because Mercury is used to influence others and help them see things your way. Spells that deal with work and career are best done on Wednesday.

THURSDAY corresponds to the planet Jupiter. It deals with idealism, expansion, and ambition. Jupiter will help you attain friendship. Thursday is a good time to do spells for career success, and situations concerned with money. Legal transactions are best dealt with during Jupiter.

FRIDAY belongs to Venus, the goddess of love. All things concerned with love, attraction, friendships, and lust come under the jurisdiction of Venus. Friday is the best time to work spells that involve sensual and sexual attraction or friendships.

SATURDAY, the last day of the week, is associated with Saturn and the first law of Karma (limitation). Magickally, Saturn is the tester and the principle of learning through trial and error. Saturn spells should be used to preserve, stabilize, and crystallize ability—the ability to discipline the self.

Correspondences for the Months of the Year

Month	Attribute	Color	Stone
January	Protection	Black	Onyx
February	Motivation	Turquoise	Aquamarine
March	Victory	Purple	Amethyst
April	Opportunity	Red	Garnet
May	Progress	Blue	Lapis Lazuli
June	Devotion	Green	Aventurine
July	Control	Yellow	Diamond
August	Unity	Brown	Agate
September	Harvest	Gold	Topaz
October	Transformation	Clear	Diamond
November	Psychic	Dark Blue	Sapphire
December	Insight	White	Chalcedony

Color Correspondences

Red:	Courage, strength, immediate action survival, lust, power
Pink:	Love, friendship, calm, emotions
Orange:	Action, attraction, selling, self-promotion, attraction
Yellow:	Communication, selling, persuasion, attraction
Green:	Love, fertility, money, luck, health, personal goals
Blue:	Creativity, tranquility, peace, perception, patience
Dark Blue:	Wisdom, self-awareness, psychic abilities, cause change
Purple:	Power, ambition, tension, spiritual development, power over others
Black:	Protection, return, cause discord, release negativity, power
Brown:	Stability, grounding, earth rites, create indecision
Gold:	Prosperity, attraction, increase wealth, money-drawing
White:	Universal color, general candle magick

Bibliography

Adkins, Lesley and Roy A. Adkins. *Dictionary of Roman Religion*. New York: Facts On File, 1996.

———. *Handbook to Life in Ancient Rome*. New York: Facts On File, 1994.

Barkin, Carol and Elizabeth James. *The Holiday Handbook*. New York: Clarion Books, 1994.

Blackburn, Bonnie and Leofranc Holford-Strevens. *The Oxford Companion to the Year*. New York: Oxford Press, 1999.

Brodie, Jan. *Earth Dance: A Year of Pagan Rituals*. London: Capal Bann Publishing, 1995.

Cohen, Hennig and Tristram Potter Coffin. *America Celebrates!* Michigan: Visible Ink Press, 1991.

Cooper, J.C. *An Illustrated Encyclopedia of Traditional Symbols*. London: Thames in Hudson, 1978.

———. *Dictionary of Festivals*. California: Harper-Collins, 1990.

Cunningham, Scott. *The Complete Book of Incense, Oils & Brews*. Minnesota: Llewellyn, 1989.

———. *Cunningham's Encyclopedia of Magical Herbs*. Minnesota: Llewellyn, 1988.

Durdin-Robertson, Lawrence. *The Year of the Goddess: A Perpetual Calendar of Festivals*. London: Aquarian Press, 1990.

Farrar, Janet, Stewart Farrar, and Gavin Bone. *The Complete Dictionary of European Gods and Goddesses.* London: Capal Bann Publishing, 2000.

Franklin, Anna and Paul Mason. *Lammas: Celebrating Fruits of the First Harvest.* Minnesota: Llewellyn Publications, 2001.

Franklin, Anna and Pamela Harvey. *The Wellspring: A Book of Seasonal Inspirations.* London: Capal Bann Publishing, 1999.

Galenorn, Yasmine. *Dancing with the Sun.* Minnesota: Llewellyn Publications, 1999.

Gordon, Leah. *The Book of Vodou: Charms and Rituals to Empower Your Life.* London: Barron's, 2000.

Green, Marian. *A Calendar of Festivals.* Massachusetts: Element Books, 1991.

Hoever, Rev. Hugo. *Lives of the Saints: For Every Day of the Year.* New York: Catholic Book Publishing Company, 1977.

Holland, Eileen. *The Wicca Handbook*. Maine: Samuel Weiser, 2000.

Hope-Simpson, Jacynth. *Covens and Cauldrons.* London: Beaver Books, 1966.

Howard, Michael. *The Sacred Ring: The Pagan Origins of British Folk Festivals & Customs.* London: Capal Bann Publishing, 1995.

Hutton, Ronald. *The Stations of the Sun: A History of the Ritual Year in Britain.* New York: Oxford University Press, 1996.

Kightly, Charles. *The Customs and Ceremonies of Britain.* London: Thames in Hudson, 1986.

Kightly, Charles. *The Perpetual Almanack of Folklore.* London: Thames in Hudson, 1987.

Leach, Maria and Jerome Fried, ed. *Funk & Wagnall's Standard Dictionary of Folklore, Mythology and Legend.* San Francisco: Harper and Row, 1972.

MacCrossan, Tadhg. *The Sacred Cauldron: Secrets of the Druids.* Minnesota: Llewellyn, 1992.

Melville, Francis. *The Book of Angels.* London: Barron's, 2001.

Moorey, Teresa and Jane Brideson. *Wheel of the Year.* London: Hodder & Stoughton, 1997.

Pagram, Beverly. *Heaven & Hearth—A Seasonal Compendium of Women's Spiritual & Domestic Lore.* London: The Women's Press Ltd., 1997.

Pennick, Nigel and Helen Field. *The God Year: Festival Days of the Sacred Male.* London: Capal Bann Publishing, 1998.

Pennick, Nigel. *The Pagan Book of Days.* Vermont: Destiny Books, 1992.

Pepper, Elizabeth and John Wilcock. *A Book of Days: Wisdom Through the Seasons.* California: Capra Press, 1996.

Rice, Edward. *Eastern Definitions.* New York: Anchor Books, 1980.

Sabrina, Lady. *Secrets of Modern Witchcraft Revealed.* New Jersey: Citadel Press, 1998.

———. *Exploring Wicca.* New Jersey: New Page Books, 2000.

———. *Wiccan Magick for Beginners.* New York: Citadel Press, 2001.

———. *Witch's Master Grimoire.* New Jersey: New Page Books, 2000.

Sacks, David. *A Dictionary of the Ancient Greek World.* New York: Oxford University Press, 1995.

Simpson, Jacqueline and Steve Roud. *A Dictionary of English Folklore.* New York: Oxford University Press, 2000.

Telesco, Patricia. *Seasons of the Sun.* Maine: Samuel Weiser, 1996.

———. *365 Goddesses: A Daily Guide to the Magic and Inspiration of the Goddess.* California: Harper San Francisco, 1998.

Index

About the Author

Lady Sabrina has been a teacher and practitioner of Wicca and the magickal arts for more than 25 years. She is an initiated Priestess of the Wiccan religion and the founder of Our Lady of Enchantment, the largest recognized seminary of Wicca in the United States (*www.wiccaseminary.org*). As a spokesperson for Wicca, Sabrina has appeared on major television talk shows, including Phil Donahue and Geraldo, and regularly conducts interviews for nationally syndicated radio. Sabrina is the author of many fine books on Wicca, including *Exploring Wicca*, *The Witches Master Grimoire*, and *Wiccan Magick for Beginners*. Sabrina lives in northern California with her three dogs, and teaches art classes in her spare time.

Other Books by Lady Sabrina

The Witches Master Grimoire
Wiccan Magick for Beginners
The Secrets of Modern Witchcraft Revealed
Cauldron of Transformation
Reclaiming the Power
Exploring Wicca

FREE INFORMATION – SPECIAL SAVINGS
Body / Mind / Spirit Titles from *New Page Books*

* Wicca *Magickal Arts *Herbalism *Alternative Therapies * Healing *Astrology *Spellcraft *Rituals *Yoga *Folk Magic *Wellness *Numerology *Meditation *Candle Magick *Celts and Druids *Shamanism *Dream Interpretation *Divination *Tarot *Palmistry *Graphology *Visualization *Supernatural *Gemstones *Aromatherapy…and more, by the authors you trust!

SELECTED TITLES INCLUDE:

*Ancient Spellcraft – Perry
*Animal Spirit – Telesco & Hall
*Celtic Astrology – Vega
*Celtic Myth and Legend - Squire; new introduction by Knight
*A Charmed Life - Telesco
*Circle of Isis – Cannon Reed
*Clan of the Goddess – Brondwin
*The Cyber Spellbook – Knight & Telesco
*Discover Yourself Through Palmreading – Robinson
*Dreams of the Goddess – Ross
*An Enchanted Life – Telesco
*Enchantments of the Heart – Morrison
*Exploring Candle Magick – Telesco
*Exploring Celtic Druidism – Knight
*Exploring Feng Shui – Mitchell with Gunning
*Exploring Meditation – Shumsky
*Exploring Scrying – Hawk
*Exploring Spellcraft - Dunwich
*Exploring Wicca - Lady Sabrina
*Faery Magick – Knight
*Gardening with the Goddess – Telesco
*The Haindl Tarot: Volume I - Pollack
*The Haindl Tarot: Volume II - Pollack

*Handwriting Analysis - Amend & Ruiz
*Healing With Crystals – Chase & Pawlik
*Healing With Gemstones – Chase & Pawlik
*Herbal Magick – Dunwich
*Karmic Tarot, 3rd Ed. - Lammey
*Magickal Astrology - Alexander
*A Medicine Woman Speaks – Moon
*Money Magick – Telesco
*The Palm – Robinson
*The Practical Pagan –Eilers
*Secrets of the Ancient Incas –Langevin
*Self-Hypnosis – Goldberg
*Tarot: A Classic Handbook for the Apprentice - Connolly
*Tarot: A New Handbook for the Apprentice - Connolly
*Tarot: The First Handbook for the Master - Connolly
*Tarot for Your Self, 2nd Ed. - Greer
*The Well-Read Witch – McColman
*Wicca Spellcraft for Men –Drew
*Master Grimoire - Lady Sabrina
* *And more!*

To be included in our *New Page Books Club* – and receive our catalog, special savings, and advance notice on upcoming titles – send your name and address to the address listed below. Or for fast service, please call 1-800-227-3371 and give the operator code #593. We look forward to hearing from you!

New Page Books
Dept. 593, 3 Tice Road
Franklin Lakes, NJ 07417

Books subject to availability.